Early praise for *Java by Comparison*

This is the book I've been waiting for since starting with intermediate Java programming courses. Without dwelling for too long on the basics, *Java by Comparison* leads you step by step to new insights on good coding practice. Instructive examples compare the do's and dont's and make it easy for beginners to get the key points. Here, the book shines and shows it's based on long-term classroom experience. Luckily, the book can be read as a textbook but is also useful as a reference. I'm looking forward to using it in my classrooms. Are you sure your style is perfect? Get it!

➤ **Dr. Guido Wirtz**
   Professor for CS/Head of Distributed Systems Group, University of Bamberg

I wish *Java by Comparison* had been there when I was getting started with programming, It's like a mentor, looking over your shoulder, and patiently helping you get your programming skills up to the next level.

➤ **Achim Weimert**
   CTO, wOndary LTD

Java by Comparison is a wonderful read for all those who want to level up their Java skills. It contains the essence of *Effective Java* and *Clean Code*, updated with JUnit 5 and Java 8.

➤ **Johannes Schwalb**
   Java Architect, uniVersa Versicherungen

The definitive guide for students to bridge the gap between the novice and the intermediate level.

➤ **Dr. Oliver Kopp**
  Postdoc, University of Stuttgart

Java by Comparison is a well-crafted quick read with good, succinct examples updated with the latest Java 8 styling. Highly recommended for Java developers a few years into their career.

➤ **Ashish Bhatia**
  Software Engineer

I think *Java by Comparison* hits a sweet spot between providing useful content and not trying to be too much. It is an easier and more directly applicable read for junior developers than *Effective Java* (the *best* Java book). Experienced developers will be seen nodding in agreement and likely learn a couple things along the ride. This will be required reading for developers.

➤ **Sebastian Larsson**
  Competence Team Lead, Cybercom Sweden

To become a software craftsman, you need to practice, practice, practice. *Java by Comparison* can accompany you during those practices. With the comparison approach, bad code to better code, it can serve as a reference during your practice hours.

➤ **Zulfikar Dharmawan**
  Software Engineer

Java by Comparison presents a number of examples on how to improve your coding skills and serves as a shortcut for beginners or intermediate programmers to become experienced programmers. The book in a sense provides a lower-level version of design patterns focusing on code structure rather than on higher-level constructs.

➤ **Dr. Martin Blom**
 Associate Professor, Karlstad University

Java by Comparison is a great read if you are looking to take your Java knowledge up another notch. I wish I could have read this book or something similar when I first started with Java; it explains a lot of topics easily that I had to learn the hard way. It is a must-read if you want to go from a good programmer to a great one.

➤ **Ramaninder Singh Jhajj**
 Big Data Engineer, Betsson Group

Well organized and full of examples, *Java by Comparison* can help you whether you are a student or a developer with years of experience.

➤ **Emanuele Origgi**
 Android Software Engineer, Funambol Inc.

With any language, once you've mastered its syntax, the next step is to learn how to use it idiomatically. Whether you're a beginner who has just started with Java or a seasoned Java developer who started out using one of its many earlier versions, I consider *Java by Comparison* a great step to become proficient in using Java well.

➤ **Stefan Tilkov**
 CEO, INNOQ

Java by Comparison

Become a Java Craftsman in 70 Examples

Simon Harrer

Jörg Lenhard

Linus Dietz

The Pragmatic Bookshelf

Raleigh, North Carolina

Many of the designations used by manufacturers and sellers to distinguish their products are claimed as trademarks. Where those designations appear in this book, and The Pragmatic Programmers, LLC was aware of a trademark claim, the designations have been printed in initial capital letters or in all capitals. The Pragmatic Starter Kit, The Pragmatic Programmer, Pragmatic Programming, Pragmatic Bookshelf, PragProg and the linking *g* device are trademarks of The Pragmatic Programmers, LLC.

Every precaution was taken in the preparation of this book. However, the publisher assumes no responsibility for errors or omissions, or for damages that may result from the use of information (including program listings) contained herein.

Our Pragmatic books, screencasts, and audio books can help you and your team create better software and have more fun. Visit us at *https://pragprog.com*.

The team that produced this book includes:

Publisher: Andy Hunt
VP of Operations: Janet Furlow
Managing Editor: Brian MacDonald
Supervising Editor: Jacquelyn Carter
Development Editor: Andrea Stewart
Copy Editor: Liz Welch
Indexing: Potomac Indexing, LLC
Layout: Gilson Graphics

For sales, volume licensing, and support, please contact *support@pragprog.com*.

For international rights, please contact *rights@pragprog.com*.

ISBN-13: 978-1-68050-287-9

Book version: P1.0—March 2018

Contents

Foreword xi
Acknowledgments xiii
Welcome! xv

1. Start Cleaning Up 1
    Avoid Unnecessary Comparisons   2
    Avoid Negations   4
    Return Boolean Expressions Directly   6
    Simplify Boolean Expressions   8
    Avoid NullPointerException in Conditionals   10
    Avoid Switch Fallthrough   12
    Always Use Braces   14
    Ensure Code Symmetry   16
    What Have You Learned?   18

2. Level Up Your Code Style 19
    Replace Magic Numbers with Constants   20
    Favor Enums Over Integer Constants   22
    Favor For-Each Over For Loops   24
    Avoid Collection Modification During Iteration 26
    Avoid Compute-Intense Operations During Iteration 28
    Group with New Lines   30
    Favor Format Over Concatenation   32
    Favor Java API Over DIY   34
    What Have You Learned?   36

3. Use Comments Wisely 37
    Remove Superfluous Comments   38
    Remove Commented-Out Code   40
    Replace Comments with Constants   42

Replace Comments with Utility Methods 44
Document Implementation Decisions 46
Document Using Examples 48
Structure JavaDoc of Packages 50
Structure JavaDoc of Classes and Interfaces 52
Structure JavaDoc of Methods 54
Structure JavaDoc of Constructors 56
What Have You Learned? 58

4. Name Things Right 59
Use Java Naming Conventions 60
Follow Getter/Setter Conventions for Frameworks 62
Avoid Single-Letter Names 64
Avoid Abbreviations 66
Avoid Meaningless Terms 68
Use Domain Terminology 70
What Have You Learned? 72

5. Prepare for Things Going Wrong 73
Fail Fast 74
Always Catch Most Specific Exception 76
Explain Cause in Message 78
Avoid Breaking the Cause Chain 80
Expose Cause in Variable 82
Always Check Type Before Cast 84
Always Close Resources 86
Always Close Multiple Resources 88
Explain Empty Catch 90
What Have You Learned? 92

6. Assert Things Going Right 93
Structure Tests Into Given-When-Then 94
Use Meaningful Assertions 96
Expected Before Actual Value 98
Use Reasonable Tolerance Values 100
Let JUnit Handle Exceptions 102
Describe Your Tests 104
Favor Standalone Tests 106
Parametrize Your Tests 108
Cover the Edge Cases 110
What Have You Learned? 112

7. **Design Your Objects** **113**
    Split Method with Boolean Parameters   114
    Split Method with Optional Parameters   116
    Favor Abstract Over Concrete Types   118
    Favor Immutable Over Mutable State   120
    Combine State and Behavior   122
    Avoid Leaking References   124
    Avoid Returning Null   126
    What Have You Learned?   128

8. **Let Your Data Flow** **129**
    Favor Lambdas Over Anonymous Classes   130
    Favor Functional Over Imperative Style   132
    Favor Method References Over Lambdas   134
    Avoid Side Effects   136
    Use Collect for Terminating Complex Streams 138
    Avoid Exceptions in Streams   140
    Favor Optional Over Null   142
    Avoid Optional Fields or Parameters   144
    Use Optionals as Streams   146
    What Have You Learned?   148

9. **Prepare for the Real World** **149**
    Use Static Code Analysis Tools   150
    Agree On the Java Format in Your Team   152
    Automate Your Build   153
    Use Continuous Integration   154
    Prepare for and Deliver Into Production   155
    Favor Logging Over Console Output   156
    Minimize and Isolate Multithreaded Code   158
    Use High-Level Concurrency Abstractions   159
    Speed Up Your Program   160
    Know Your Falsehoods   162
    What Have You Learned?   164

    Bibliography **165**
    Index **167**

Foreword

We can learn a great deal from observing others. As a woman makes entry through a door, she momentarily holds it open for the person approaching behind. That's her expression of empathy and humanity. While she is focused on moving forward, she also cares about the person behind and wants to make their journey at least a bit pleasant. That person behind is a total stranger, they may never meet again, and yet she showed benevolence.

Programming is a passion for many, but it also deeply involves empathy and humanity.

When we write code, there is always someone behind us. Sometimes it's ourselves after a few hours, days, weeks, or months. But it's often a colleague who comes around to make changes to the code, fix a bug, add a feature, extend the software. To make the code easier for that person to maintain is far beyond an act of benevolence. It's part of being a professional. It's part of practicing the craft.

Writing code is easy. Writing good-quality code takes effort, discipline, and a lot of practice. There are many different definitions for code quality. Here's mine:

Code Quality
> The quality of code is inversely proportional to the amount of effort to understand it.

Good code is transparent. It makes the logic obvious to readers so they can get on with their work. Poor code is opaque and hides the logic. The reader has to spend time and effort to figure out the details from badly written code.

When we sit down to program a feature or a particular logic, we're focused deeply on getting it to work. Programming is a series of mini experiments and discoveries. We often have to devise solutions and approaches to implement the problem at hand. Creating code is but only the first step. Code is written once, but it is read and evolved many times. If the code we create is of poor quality, even if it appears to function flawlessly, we have increased the cost of ownership of that code over time.

Most of the programmers hired to write code will deliver working software. The difference between average programmers and amazing ones is how easy it is for others to follow their work.

Writing good-quality code is a skill. As with any skill, in order to acquire and improve, we have to make a conscious effort, get critiqued, and take the time to learn. With continuous effort, writing good-quality code becomes second nature and will begin to seem effortless. The journey is hard, but at the same time, it's a wonderful learning experience. Part of that learning can come from reading great books, like the one you're about to begin.

In the three-plus decades I have been programming, I have made most of the mistakes mentioned in this book. I spend a lot of time these days reviewing code written by students and also by professionals in the industry. I see both students and professionals making many of the same mistakes. As you read this book, you will quickly relate to mistakes that you may have already made. The first step in solving a problem is realizing it. The authors of this book have done a wonderful job of guiding us through the smells, the issues, and the consequences of each bad piece of code. Then they show us ways to avoid the mess, how to write quality code, and the benefits we derive from the better quality.

I urge you not to rush through this book. Sometimes we have to slow down to gain speed. As you move through the book, take time to read each piece of bad code and spend some time identifying things that are wrong. Jot them down. Then read through the authors' explanations. This will help with better absorption and also help you to develop a sense for quality and style. Then, think through possible solutions, again, before jumping in to read the presented solution and the reasoning.

Writing code is fun. Writing code that is easier to understand and evolve is pure bliss. It is truly a pleasure to see a book written to help aspiring programmers become respectable professionals. Let Simon, Jörg, and Linus be your guides—you're in good hands.

Let's turn programming into a wonderful craft.

Dr. Venkat Subramaniam
President, Agile Developer, Inc. March 2018

Acknowledgments

Books can take a long time from the initial idea to the printing. This one started during the 2016 UEFA European Championship, the European championship in soccer. At that time, Simon and Linus were teaching a programming course called "Advanced Java Programming" at the University of Bamberg—a course that Simon and Jörg had developed together and taught for five years.

With student enrollment numbers rising, it became quite arduous to provide detailed written feedback on the code quality of the students' programming assignments. Since code quality can turn into an obsession, Simon and Linus were discussing this problem while watching soccer matches. It was obvious that despite their talent, students were making the same mistakes over and over. Eventually, the guys came up with the solution: a collection of common issues. Instead of explaining the problem over and over, they gave each mistake a name, provided one condensed code solution, and explained everything the students needed to know about it. Now they could just refer students to these items, saving much time and even improving the feedback quality!

The idea of *Java by Comparison* was born, and relaxed evenings watching soccer on TV quickly turned into hacking and drafting code comparisons. Eventually, Simon and Linus realized that this might actually make a helpful programming book, and they got Jörg on board. A draft proposal for Pragmatic Bookshelf was prepared, submitted, accepted, and then the real work started…

This book wouldn't be in its current shape without contributions by many people. First and foremost, we are grateful to Professor Dr. Guido Wirtz for bringing us together at his Distributed Systems Group and providing the supportive environment in which we could grow (and do our PhDs) and such a book could come into being. We'd like to thank Venkat Subramaniam, whose excellent books we used in our courses, for writing the foreword to this book.

We're also grateful to all the people who gave us the permission to add their quotes to our chapter openings. In particular, thanks go to David Heinemeier Hanson, Martin Fowler, Sean Parent, Steve McConnell, Phil Karlton, Alan J. Perlis, Dave Thomas, Andy Hunt, David Wheeler, Michael Feathers, and Tom Cargill.

On top of that, numerous people volunteered to read the book and supply us with excellent technical reviews before and during the beta phase of the book. They pointed out errors, suggested improvements, and made this book much better overall. Thank you, Cedric Röck, Oliver Kopp, Michael Träger, Jan Boockmann, Venkat Subramaniam (again), Matthias Geiger, Johannes Schwalb, Hendrick Cech, Klaus Stein, Ivo Balbaert, Al Scherer, Philipp Neugebauer, Emanuele Origgi, Ashish Bhatia, Zulfikar Dharmawan, Achim Weimert, Sebastian Larsson, Ramaninder Singh Jhajj, Martin Blom, and Marcus Biel.

Last but not least, we want to express our gratitude to the folks at Pragmatic Bookshelf. Special thanks go to our editor, Andrea Stewart. Thanks for your patience, for endlessly rephrasing passive sentences into active voice, and for helping us get used to the pragmatic style of writing. But there are more people in the background that have made this book a reality. Many thanks to Susannah Pfalzer, Jackie Carter, Katie Dvorak, Brian MacDonald, and Andy Hunt!

Welcome!

We agree with David Heinemeier Hanson.

If you propose a programming technique, you should be able to demonstrate as concisely as possible how your proposal is better than what was there before. The before/after approach puts all the facts on the table: you can directly compare the new code to the old code. Only then can you make an informed decision about which one's better.

The same holds true when you're learning how to program. Comparing good code to bad code is really helpful when you're trying to figure out how to code in Java.

We used to teach programming at a university for over six years. After a few lectures, there were *always* a few students asking us, "How can I improve my coding skills further?" These students excelled in their programming assignments, anyway, so we gave them the default advice: "Read code from professionals."

Honestly, our advice wasn't very helpful. There's plenty of code out in the open source software world, but it's hard to tell where to start. Beginners get quickly overwhelmed with the complexity of professional code in real-life projects. And how do you know if a piece of source code is actually of high quality? Even if it is, how can someone with only a few months of programming experience distinguish it from a flawed hack?

That's where this book comes into play. It's a companion that guides your reading in the right direction. We'll help you learn how to write good Java code by comparing pieces of bad code with good code. And be assured: we've seen our fair share of bad and good code over the years, reviewing code written by students in academia, professionals in industry, and contributors in open source projects.

This brings us back to the before/after approach. In this book, we'll provide you with 70 before/after code snippets. These snippets will help any beginner in Java programming to improve. We identified these snippets during our time of teaching Java to undergraduates at the university. They're all based on code we faced when correcting our students' programming assignments.

Our approach in this book is simple: Given a code snippet, we'll first explain what's wrong and why. Then, we'll show you how you can transform the code into a better solution.

Who Should Read This Book

This book is for people who are learning to program in Java at a beginner or intermediate level. It's also a classroom resource for teachers who coach new developers in their journey to become programmers. Here, we're giving you tips and tricks based on more recent Java 8[1] syntax for resource handling, functional programming, or testing.

You should read this book after you've learned the basic Java syntax—after you're able to write small programs with conditions and loops and you know the basics of object-oriented programming. You should be able to write code that compiles, runs, and solves small tasks like FizzBuzz (see *Are You Ready? Try the Self-Assessment*, on page xvii). You should be able to implement simple algorithms, and you should know how to use basic data structures like a list, queue, stack, or map. And obviously, you should be having fun while doing all that!

If you feel a deep satisfaction when you solve a complicated problem, then that's an excellent start. But of course, you also know that there's still a lot to learn. When you reflect on your skills and you have to confess that you don't have a lot of experience in programming in Java (or even programming in general), then you can get the maximum benefit out of this book. This means that you probably haven't yet developed a sense for *clean code* and the best practices an experienced developer applies.

It's about time to change this!

Of course, if you already know more advanced books on code quality, readability, maintainability, and clean code in Java, such as *Effective Java [Blo18]* and *Clean Code [Mar08]*, then you've already come a long way. Nevertheless, you can still find something new here and there.

---

1. We know that Oracle already released Java 9. Rest assured that everything in this book is still valid in Java 9.

Teaching Clean Code Using This Book

If you teach programming to newcomers as a senior developer at a company, you're certainly aware of the best practices we'll go over in this book. You might even disagree with some, depending on what you are working on. Still, this book can make your life easier when training a junior developer—just use it as a reference. When you spot problems in your apprentice's code, point her to the corresponding item in this book. Your student can read a concise and simple example for the problem you're hinting at, as well as how to get to the solution of the problem. At the very least, this saves you time because you won't have to write an explanation yourself.

Our experience in developing teaching concepts for Java learners in their second to third year can also be useful for teaching in academia. This book is the product of our combined knowledge of over fifteen years of teaching Java to undergraduate college students in an advanced course with focus on code quality. It might not teach Java from the ground up, but it can accompany basically any course that involves programming tasks. In particular, you can use the book as a reference when you asses student code, as we've described in a workshop paper: *Teaching Clean Code [DMHL18]*.

Are You Ready? Try the Self-Assessment

If you're a new programmer, we suggest that you do a short self-assessment to see if you're ready for the material in this book: the FizzBuzz Test (see the *Fizz Buzz Test*[2] or *Using FizzBuzz to Find Developers who Grok Coding*[3]). Some employers use this test in job interviews to determine if an applicant can program at all. The task goes like this:

> Write a Java program that prints the numbers from 1 to 100 to the console. But for multiples of three, print *Fizz* instead of the number and for multiples of five, print *Buzz*. For numbers that are multiples of both three and five, print *FizzBuzz*.

To make the test more interesting, we'll extend it a bit here by making sure that you can apply object orientation and use classes and interfaces as well. You should implement the FizzBuzz algorithm in a class called ConsoleBasedFizzBuzz, which implements a FizzBuzz interface. This interface provides a method that takes the first and last numbers to print as arguments. In the main method of a separate Main class, you should use the FizzBuzz interface with its ConsoleBasedFizzBuzz implementation to count from 1 up to the value passed from the console. Here, you'll see the outlined structure in a short template.

---

2. http://c2.com/cgi/wiki?FizzBuzzTest
3. https://imranontech.com/2007/01/24/using-fizzbuzz-to-find-developers-who-grok-coding/

```java
interface FizzBuzz {
    void print(int from, int to);
}

class ConsoleBasedFizzBuzz implements FizzBuzz {
    // TODO implement FizzBuzz interface
}

class Main {
    // TODO use a main method
    // TODO print fizz buzz from 1 to max
    // TODO max is passed from the console
}
```

You should be able to finish this exercise in about *15 minutes*. One of the links we listed also contains solutions to the FizzBuzz challenge that you can compare to your own. If you can do it, then you're ready to get the most out of this book. If not, don't worry! Keep reading anyway. It might take you a little longer, and you might have a harder time understanding a comparison here and there. But if you practice programming by solving small exercises like the ones in this book, you'll get on track quickly.

Many good resources are available online for practicing your programming skills and getting feedback on your code. Have a look at codewars.com[4] or cyber-dojo.[5] These pages let you train your programming skills in various levels of difficulty. If you have a mathematical background, you'll find solving the problems of Project Euler[6] quite appealing.

If, on the other hand, you find the FizzBuzz test terribly easy, and your solution compiles and runs within seconds, be aware that you might already know some of the practices that we outline in this book. You can still get something out of it, of course. We've made all the comparisons self-contained. So feel free to jump around and skip the parts that you already know.

Why Read This Book?

Every developer has a number of requirements in mind that she considers prerequisites for *good* or *clean code*. As long as a piece of code doesn't violate any of these requirements, it qualifies as *good* or *clean* from the viewpoint of the developer. Different people have different requirements. And programming languages differ, of course. But still, for a given language, there's typically a set of *"core"* requirements and best practices. These are aspects that the

---

4.   https://www.codewars.com/?language=java
5.   http://cyber-dojo.org/
6.   https://projecteuler.net

community of developers recognizes and accepts, even if they aren't written down explicitly. In this book, we're trying to provide you—someone who might not yet be aware of many of the practices in the Java community—with a set of best practices for clean code in Java.

As a beginner, your list of requirements for good Java code might be as short as this one:

- The code must compile.
- The output must be correct.

These items are about the functional correctness of your program, but they don't tell much about the quality of your code. An experienced programmer cares about a lot more than that, and her checklist is much longer. She just needs a quick glance at a piece of code to detect flaws, bad naming, hard-to-test methods, inconsistencies, bad practices, and much more.

The aim of this book is to train your brain to internalize more checklist items, helping you on your way to becoming an experienced and professional programmer. Each of the items in this book represents such a checklist item.

Conventions Used in This Book

Throughout the book, we use a specific structure for explaining each checklist item. We call it "comparison," and we zealously stick to it.

Each comparison has a catchy name. This helps you to memorize it for your mental checklist. Take a look at the table of contents—it acts as the checklist of this book. The name of a comparison makes it easier to talk to other people about what you've read. We've named the comparisons in a way that encourages you to consider them as a recommendation. You can also put "You should" in front of a comparison name—for example: You should *avoid unnecessary comparisons*. For the upcoming example, we selected the catchy name "Never Trust Your Input."

Directly after the name, we'll present a snippet of code and highlight a problem in it. This can be a block of several lines or just a single one, like this:

```java
class HelloWorld {

    public static void main(String[] args) {
        System.out.println("Hello " + args[0]);
    }
}
```

In these code snippets, we want to distract you as little as possible. That's why we have to shorten the code a little bit to get to the essentials:

1. We leave out import statements and package declarations. The downloadable code[7] contains those declarations, of course—it would not compile otherwise.

2. We avoid visibility modifiers, such as public or private, unless they're explicitly required.

Following the code snippet, we explain to you what the problem is. On the way, we provide references to further reading, such as JavaDoc, related items, or web pages.

Then, we show you the code of a solution and highlight the solution-specific parts.

```java
class HelloWorld {

    public static void main(String[] arguments) {
        if (isEmpty(arguments)) {
            return;
        }

        System.out.println("Hello " + arguments[0]);
    }

    private static boolean isEmpty(String[] array) {
        return (array == null) || (array.length == 0);
    }
}
```

Sometimes, there's very little difference between the problem code and the solution. Sometimes, there's a lot of difference. Either way, the snippets themselves should already teach you something—a certain style that helps you to produce better code. We deliberately keep each comparison on two pages. The left-hand side (or first page) shows the problem, and the right-hand side (or second page) shows the solution. This way, you can always compare both code snippets without having to flip pages back and forth. This makes it a lot easier to learn what an item is about. If you're reading this book as a PDF with Adobe Reader, make sure you've enabled two-page view and that the cover page is shown—it's almost like reading from the printed book.

---

7. https://pragprog.com/titles/javacomp/source_code

Why Should I Learn This? There Are Static Code Analysis Tools...

You might be thinking that you already have static code analysis tools, such as Checkstyle,[8] FindBugs,[9] SpotBugs,[10] Error Prone,[11] and PMD,[12] that detect flaws in your code. So why should you keep reading this?

That's true for some, but it's not true for all the problems in this book. We'd love to see a tool that can *automatically* and *correctly* assess the concerns in your code. The existing tools are good, but they're not perfect. Think of them as rigorous, intolerant, nitpicky robots that were taught a set of rules and seek any violation. They can't understand that sometimes there are circumstances where you must violate a rule to improve the code. To use them successfully, they need to be fine-tuned, and that requires in-depth knowledge about code quality and the project at hand.[13] But even then, they can never beat an experienced programmer, although they can help so that some issues aren't missed.

That's good news, because it means that as an experienced programmer, your skills will be in high demand. Tools can check for a lot of things, but they often lack a detailed explanation for why something was detected. And they rarely show you how to solve a specific issue. Oftentimes, the solution to an issue isn't apparent from the warning of a detection tool, and it's rare that you can correct the code automatically. You have to do this manually, and that process is error prone—especially if you're still learning Java. As a new programmer, the tools won't guide you to a sensible correction. That's where this book can help you. We'll raise your awareness for common programming errors that many people make when learning Java.

How to Read This Book

If you're in your first year of Java, we suggest you read the book from start to finish. It starts with rather basic comparisons first, but then we'll advance to more challenging topics, like testing, object-oriented design, and functional programming in Java. If you're more experienced, you can probably skip the first two chapters and dig right into the more specialized topics.

---

8. http://checkstyle.sourceforge.net/
9. http://findbugs.sourceforge.net/
10. https://github.com/spotbugs/spotbugs
11. http://errorprone.info/
12. https://pmd.github.io/
13. Keep in mind: A fool with a tool is still a fool!

Here's a brief outline:

- In Chapter 1, *Start Cleaning Up*, on page 1 we'll give you general advice on how to write correct code that's readable and understandable. We'll touch on a lot of things related to the basic Java syntax, such as conditions and braces.

- In Chapter 2, *Level Up Your Code Style*, on page 19 we'll discuss a few more advanced coding concepts and problems, such as iteration, formatting, and using the Java API.

- Chapter 3, *Use Comments Wisely*, on page 37 is about documenting code well. We'll give you some advice on how to write comments and when you should get rid of them.

- In Chapter 4, *Name Things Right*, on page 59 we'll explain how you assign proper and concise names to code elements in Java that other programmers will easily understand.

- Chapter 5, *Prepare for Things Going Wrong*, on page 73 will make you aware of how you should handle exceptions in Java.

- Chapter 6, *Assert Things Going Right*, on page 93 gives you advice on how to write good unit tests with JUnit5.

- Chapter 7, *Design Your Objects*, on page 113 outlines object-oriented design principles.

- Chapter 8, *Let Your Data Flow*, on page 129 focuses on functional programming in Java using lambda expressions.

- Finally, Chapter 9, *Prepare for the Real World*, on page 149 directs you to tons of material on building, releasing, and maintaining your software in the real world.

So let's move on and have fun!

Online Resources

This book has its own web page at www.pragprog.com.[14] There, you can get in touch with us in the discussion forum,[15] post errata,[16] or download the source code[17] of this book.

---

14. https://pragprog.com/titles/javacomp
15. http://forums.pragprog.com/forums/javacomp
16. http://pragprog.com/titles/javacomp/errata
17. https://pragprog.com/titles/javacomp/source_code

Get Ready for Your Mission to Mars

As a beginner or intermediate programmer, getting a sense for good and clean code that others will recognize as such might appear to you as something far, far away, a goal almost unreachable—a long journey, full of unexpected problems and unknown experiences. It's a bit like traveling through space to a destination that humanity hasn't reached yet: a journey to Mars! That was sort of how we felt when we started to learn programming many years ago.

We've written the code in this book with the theme of a Mars mission, so all the code examples have something spacey about them. But the real reason is that we don't want to distract you from the problem in a code snippet with the setting that the code is in. We used the astronaut theme to give you a better read, avoid meaningless variable names like x and y, or the umpteenth inheritance hierarchy from animals to mammals to cats. (We have nothing against cats—we just think they're overused in teaching material.)

Our comparisons are based on code and coding problems that we've found that a beginner or intermediate programmer often runs into when she's learning to program. We've extracted the underlying problems and put them into the domain of space travel so it's easier to imagine the context around them.

We can't guarantee that you'll become an astronaut after reading this book, but we're very confident that you'll be a better programmer. So fasten your seatbelt, and onward into (programmer) space!

Any fool can write code that a computer can understand. Good
programmers write code that humans can understand.

> Martin Fowler

CHAPTER 1

Start Cleaning Up

Have you ever looked back at a piece of code you wrote several months ago and wondered what you were thinking? Could any of your colleagues understand it within a reasonable amount of time? Writing readable code is an essential skill for a programmer. In fact, it's one of your most important communication skills—it's your public relations agent and your calling card. It says everything people need to know about your skills as a programmer, and it quickly reveals whether you're a novice or an expert.

The truth is in the code. Forget the developer's intentions and the promises in the documentation. All a computer can do is what's instructed in code. The compiler takes the Java code and produces byte code—a machine representation based on a variety of strictly enforced rules. If the code obeys those rules, it compiles. If not, your screen fills with error messages. Simple as that.

Compilers can process any valid piece of Java code, but you can't say the same for humans. Writing code that's easy for humans to read and understand is much harder than writing code that compiles. So that's what we're starting with in this chapter: writing expert code that's easy to understand. We'll show you some tricks that make your code more readable, such as why you should avoid unnecessary comparisons and negations and how to simplify Boolean expressions.

Conveniently, code that's easy to understand also contains fewer bugs. By the time you finish this chapter, you'll be able to write better code that contains fewer bugs. You'll stay clear of NullPointerExceptions in conditional expressions and you'll be aware of some infamous bug types, such as the switch fallthrough or the GOTO FAIL bug. You'll also learn about general design principles, such as code symmetry. Let's get started!

Avoid Unnecessary Comparisons

```
class Laboratory {

    Microscope microscope;

    Result analyze(Sample sample) {
        if (microscope.isInorganic(sample) == true) {
            return Result.INORGANIC;
        } else {
            return analyzeOrganic(sample);
        }
    }

    private Result analyzeOrganic(Sample sample) {
        if (microscope.isHumanoid(sample) == false) {
            return Result.ALIEN;
        } else {
            return Result.HUMANOID;
        }
    }
}
```

The first logical conditions you learned to write probably consisted of integers and comparison operators, and a beginner might use that same way of implementing conditions with boolean values. But those comparisons are completely unnecessary—they're like noise in your code.

Here you can see code for a Laboratory component, which analyzes a Sample through conditions in two nested if-else blocks.

The code explicitly compares boolean return values to boolean primitive types (true and false). This is an anti-pattern that you can often find in code written by beginners.

If you build logical conditions with data types other than boolean, for example with integers, you need to compare them to actual values (e.g., myNumber == 25, input > 0). But you don't need to do that for boolean variables or return types.

Instead, you already have boolean expressions to work with. There's no need to compare them to boolean primitives. The comparisons clutter up the code and make it just a little harder to read.

Most of the time, you'll find that it's straightforward to get rid of such unnecessary comparisons. Not only will you have less code, but it will also be easier to read.

Now check out how straightforward this code is without those comparisons.

```
class Laboratory {

    Microscope microscope;

    Result analyze(Sample sample) {
        if (microscope.isInorganic(sample)) {
            return Result.INORGANIC;
        } else {
            return analyzeOrganic(sample);
        }
    }

    private Result analyzeOrganic(Sample sample) {
        if (!microscope.isHumanoid(sample)) {
            return Result.ALIEN;
        } else {
            return Result.HUMANOID;
        }
    }
}
```

Here, we removed the comparisons to boolean primitives. In the case of laboratory.isHumanoid(sample), we had to negate the expression to retain the semantics. But otherwise, the code is unchanged. You can now read the condition expressions a little more easily.

Any compiler would perform such a removal out-of-the-box. There's probably no difference between the two snippets in terms of the actual execution. The benefit here lies entirely in the readability of the code. It's a small fix in some simple code, but imagine you're working with a large code base—every little improvement in readability helps!

Thinking about *Avoid Negations*, on page 4, you could improve the conditions even further. So read on!

Multiple Returns vs. Single Return per Method

Countless developer hours have been invested (read: wasted) to discuss, if it's better to have a single return statement or multiple ones within a method. There's no ultimate right or wrong. Every return statement marks a point of exit from a method. A single point of exit makes for a more structured flow of control; you always know where it'll end. But sometimes you want to exit a method early—for example, when the input parameters are invalid. Here, we use multiple returns because it requires fewer lines of code—and space is always limited in a book. In your code, try to see if you need an early exit, and if you do, use multiple returns.

Avoid Negations

```
class Laboratory {

    Microscope microscope;

    Result analyze(Sample sample) {
        if (microscope.isInorganic(sample)) {
            return Result.INORGANIC;
        } else {
            return analyzeOrganic(sample);
        }
    }

    private Result analyzeOrganic(Sample sample) {
        if (!microscope.isHumanoid(sample)) {
            return Result.ALIEN;
        } else {
            return Result.HUMANOID;
        }
    }
}
```

Has anyone ever told you to "think positively"? Turns out, positive expressions are better in your code than negative ones because they're often easier to grasp and they take up slightly less space.

The problem code shown here is another variant of the Laboratory component. It provides two methods that take a Sample and return a Result. There's nothing obviously wrong with the code. It'll fulfill its purpose, but it's more complex than necessary.

Consider the conditions of the if statements: Both express a negating condition. The first one tests if a sample isInorganic(). The second one even uses the Boolean operator for negation: the exclamation mark '!'.

In most cases, you'll find it easier to understand positive expressions when you read code. A negated expression adds one extra layer of indirection. Instead of a simple "X does apply," you have to grasp an additional token: "X does *not* apply."

This extra token is often unnecessary. Although it seems like a minor change, every tiny bit of simplification helps for more complex expressions (those that you'll find in real code).

Remember: Everybody likes no negations.

Now, take a look at the simplified version:

```
class Laboratory {

    Microscope microscope;

    Result analyze(Sample sample) {
        if (microscope.isOrganic(sample)) {
            return analyzeOrganic(sample);
        } else {
            return Result.INORGANIC;
        }
    }

    private Result analyzeOrganic(Sample sample) {
        if (microscope.isHumanoid(sample)) {
            return Result.HUMANOID;
        } else {
            return Result.ALIEN;
        }
    }
}
```

We changed the code only slightly, but that already has an effect. Instead of isInorganic(), we're calling isOrganic(), which has a positive wording instead of a negative one. That is, we have to switch the bodies of the if and else blocks.

When it comes to the second part, we're calling the same method, isHumanoid(), but we eliminated the negation. This is a real simplification of the code. Again, it means that we have to switch the bodies of the if and else blocks.

All in all, these changes are quite simple and you might wonder: why should I bother? You should bother because it improves the understandability of the code and comes at virtually no cost. You don't usually have to add further lines of code. All you have to do is re-sort existing parts of the code and you'll see an improvement. It's an opportunity that's too good to let go!

Sometimes, however, you need the appropriate methods, like the isOrganic() instead of isInorganic() here. If the code you're calling comes from a third-party library, you might not have the option to invoke different methods. But when you control it, don't shy away from adding that method to the appropriate class—the few lines of code are worth their characters, because they make your code clearer in other places. In the long run you'll end up with less code, since such methods reduce code duplication and can be reused in other parts of the program. From our experience, it's best to get rid of the negative method completely—no need to maintain two similar methods.

Return Boolean Expressions Directly

```java
class Astronaut {

    String name;
    int missions;

    boolean isValid() {
        if (missions < 0 || name == null || name.trim().isEmpty()) {
            return false;
        } else {
            return true;
        }
    }
}
```

Next, let's look at another way you can cut clutter in your code. In this case, we don't need the if statement to pursue our goals. Let's find out why.

You can see a typical validation method in the snippet. The method checks a couple of attributes of an object, an integer and a String.

The integer attribute refers to a number of missions. This number shouldn't be negative.

The String attribute shouldn't be null; otherwise we risk that a NullPointerException crashes the execution at some point.

Additionally, it should not be empty, because every Astronaut should have an actual name. The call to name.trim() removes all kinds of preceding or trailing space characters, such as white spaces or tabs. If there's something left after the call to trim(), it'll be an actual sequence of characters.

There's no functional error in the code. The problem, as is so often the case, is that the code is more complex and less readable than it could be. More precisely, the if statement is entirely unnecessary. It's clutter code that only distracts from the actual semantics.

Let's see what we can do about it! The key is the return type of our method: boolean. Because of this, we don't have to wrap everything in an if statement—we can return the value right away, like this:

```
class Astronaut {

    String name;
    int missions;

    boolean isValid() {
        return missions >= 0 && name != null && !name.trim().isEmpty();
    }
}
```

This change removes a level of indentation and branching. The method is now very concise and much easier to read!

We condensed the five lines of the if statement into a single line of code. To retain the same semantics, we had to apply Boolean arithmetic to the condition. Essentially, we applied De Morgan's laws[1] and negated the condition. Here's a quick definition of these famous laws, which you'll need often:

```
!A && !B == !(A || B) // true
!A || !B == !(A && B) // true
```

There are times when the condition is more complex than this one. If this is the case, you should think about breaking it into smaller chunks. Our advice is to capture parts of a condition with variables that have meaningful names. Consider the following example:

```
boolean isValid() {
    boolean isValidMissions = missions >= 0;
    boolean isValidName = name != null && !name.trim().isEmpty();
    return isValidMissions && isValidName;
}
```

As a rule of thumb, you should consider such a simplification if you combine more than two different conditions. If you need parts of the condition elsewhere, consider putting them into separate methods, as explained in *Simplify Boolean Expressions*, on page 8.

Note that the solution depicted here only works with boolean return types.

---

1. https://en.wikipedia.org/wiki/De_Morgan%27s_laws

Simplify Boolean Expressions

```
class SpaceShip {

    Crew crew;
    FuelTank fuelTank;
    Hull hull;
    Navigator navigator;
    OxygenTank oxygenTank;

    boolean willCrewSurvive() {
        return hull.holes == 0 &&
                fuelTank.fuel >= navigator.requiredFuelToEarth() &&
                oxygenTank.lastsFor(crew.size) > navigator.timeToEarth();
    }
}
```

Boolean expressions that combine multiple conditions are often hard to understand and easy to get wrong. But you can make them easier with a few simple tricks.

As in the previous comparison, you can see an example of a validation method. The condition is more complex than the previous one, but it's already condensed in a single return statement according to *Return Boolean Expressions Directly*, on page 6.

The sheer size of the condition makes it hard to understand. It spans over several lines of code and combines checks from five different objects. Due to its size, it's easy to introduce a fault when you have to change a part of it. But even before changing it, you'll probably spend valuable programming time to grasp its meaning.

When you have to combine several conditions into a single check, it's better to group them in some way. A good grouping depends on the semantics of the condition, and you can try to group by topics or level of abstractions.

Within a method, you should combine statements that are on a similar level of abstraction. Ideally, a higher-level method should call methods of the *next* lower level.

Brackets Can Help, Too

Boolean conditions can get tricky, especially when they lack brackets. Many developers, and we count ourselves in this group, don't internalize the precedence of Boolean operators and have to think for a moment to determine if x && y || z means (x && y) || z or x && (x || z). Or did you know that && is always evaluated before || ?

Here, the method willCrewSurvive() verifies each low-level detail in the same condition. Can you think of a level of abstraction in between? How about this:

```
class SpaceShip {

    Crew crew;
    FuelTank fuelTank;
    Hull hull;
    Navigator navigator;
    OxygenTank oxygenTank;

    boolean willCrewSurvive() {
        boolean hasEnoughResources = hasEnoughFuel() && hasEnoughOxygen();
        return hull.isIntact() && hasEnoughResources;
    }

    private boolean hasEnoughOxygen() {
        return oxygenTank.lastsFor(crew.size) > navigator.timeToEarth();
    }

    private boolean hasEnoughFuel() {
        return fuelTank.fuel >= navigator.requiredFuelToEarth();
    }
}
```

Wow, a lot has changed here! The willCrewSurvive() method is still present, but now it calls other methods and aggregates their return values.

First, we have added a boolean variable that bundles similar aspects together by their topic: depletable resources. We also gave it a meaningful name, hasEnoughResources. The variable combines the results of two method calls, hasEnoughOxygen() and hasEnoughFuel(). You'll find the actual details of the conditions inside these two methods.

Next, we've combined the variable hasEnoughResources with the last missing piece of the original condition, hull.holes == 0. We, however, use the method hull.isIntact() from the Hull class instead. It already has a meaningful name so there's no real reason to store it in another boolean variable.

Although there are more lines of code now, we've improved the understandability of the code a lot. You no longer need to grasp one large condition at once. Thanks to the grouping, you can do it step by step. Plus, the names of variables and methods communicate the intended result. Each method on its own is simple and comprehensible at one glance.

Avoid NullPointerException in Conditionals

```
class Logbook {

    void writeMessage(String message, Path location) throws IOException {
        if (Files.isDirectory(location)) {
            throw new IllegalArgumentException("The path is invalid!");
        }
        if (message.trim().equals("") || message == null) {
            throw new IllegalArgumentException("The message is invalid!");
        }
        String entry = LocalDate.now() + ": " + message;
        Files.write(location, Collections.singletonList(entry),
                StandardCharsets.UTF_8, StandardOpenOption.CREATE,
                StandardOpenOption.APPEND);
    }
}
```

The first exception that beginners in Java typically see is the NullPointerException. It's triggered if you call a method or access an attribute on a reference that is null. To prevent such problems, you should validate method arguments. But be sure to do so in the right order!

The Logbook in this code snippet writes messages into a file. We organize log messages into specific files on the filesystem, which we indicate by the location argument. It's important that messages are correct, so we need to perform parameter validation.

The current version of the method already performs some validation. Unfortunately, it has two serious problems. First of all, the method doesn't check for null references properly. If location is null, the call to Files.isDirectory() will fail with an undocumented NullPointerException. The same happens for the second condition if message is null, because we check for message.equals("") first.

When you validate arguments, you have to mind the order: first check for null and only then for domain-specific "illegal" values. We recommend that you check for common default values like empty strings or empty lists first, and only then conduct more specific checks.

Passing null into a method as an argument is really bad style—it means that this method can also function without this parameter. If this is indeed the case, refactor the method into two: one with the parameter and one without. Be aware that a parameter being null usually indicates a programming error on the calling side.

Here's what a proper validation would look like.

```java
class Logbook {

    void writeMessage(String message, Path location) throws IOException {
        if (message == null || message.trim().isEmpty()) {
            throw new IllegalArgumentException("The message is invalid!");
        }
        if (location == null || Files.isDirectory(location)) {
            throw new IllegalArgumentException("The path is invalid!");
        }

        String entry = LocalDate.now() + ": " + message;
        Files.write(location, Collections.singletonList(entry),
                StandardCharsets.UTF_8, StandardOpenOption.CREATE,
                StandardOpenOption.APPEND);
    }
}
```

We've resolved all issues in the new version: First, we check all arguments for null values. After that, we check for domain-specific restrictions.

Also, we've changed the order of the checks to reflect the order of the arguments in the method signature. This is a good practice, since a proper ordering of parameter validations improves the flow of reading. You're also less likely to forget to validate one of the parameters. Finally, we've used a built-in method to check if a String is empty.

You might ask yourself: Is this level of parameter validation always necessary? It's not.

As a rule of thumb, you need parameter validation for public, protected, and default methods. That's because any part of the code can access them, and you might not control how this happens.

In contrast, when you build private methods, you're able to ensure that you never pass null into them. So in this case, you don't need to perform as much validation.

File Open Options

You might wonder what these StandardOpenOptions mean. They specify the behavior of the Files.write() method. The names are pretty self-explanatory, but you should be aware that you can combine them.

This is useful, because we don't have to bother if the file we want to APPEND to already exists on the filesystem if the CREATE flag is set, too.

Avoid Switch Fallthrough

```java
class BoardComputer {

    CruiseControl cruiseControl;

    void authorize(User user) {
        Objects.requireNonNull(user);
        switch (user.getRank()) {
            case UNKNOWN:
                cruiseControl.logUnauthorizedAccessAttempt();
            case ASTRONAUT:
                cruiseControl.grantAccess(user);
                break;
            case COMMANDER:
                cruiseControl.grantAccess(user);
                cruiseControl.grantAdminAccess(user);
                break;
        }
    }
}
```

Some programming language constructs are infamous because of all the bugs they've caused over the years. One of them is the switch, and you should be careful when you use it.

The method authorizeUser() you see here validates its parameters and checks for a null reference. It uses Objects.requireNonNull(), a handy parameter validation method from the Java API, which triggers an exception for null input. But authorizeUser() still contains a classic bug: the switch fallthrough.

The bug is in the first case of the switch statement. There's no break statement at the end of the case. This means that the switch just continues to the next case—it *falls through* and will always execute cruiseControl.grantAccess().

The switch statement is infamous for this behavior. It always continues execution until it reaches a break statement or the end of the block. You're going to find these execution semantics for the switch in any C-style language. Also, Java inherited it from C.

The switch behaves the way it does because this allows you to write code that's a little more compact and requires fewer characters, you can avoid evaluating a few condition expressions this way. And since Java 7, the switch statement even supports strings in addition to integers, characters, and enums.

But over the years, it has done more harm than good, and quite a few bugs resulted from forgotten break statements. In the rare case where a missing break is intentional, you should leave a comment!

Take a look at a bug-free version of the code.

```
class BoardComputer {

    CruiseControl cruiseControl;

    void authorize(User user) {
        Objects.requireNonNull(user);
        switch (user.getRank()) {
            case UNKNOWN:
                cruiseControl.logUnauthorizedAccessAttempt();
                break;
            case ASTRONAUT:
                cruiseControl.grantAccess(user);
                break;
            case COMMANDER:
                cruiseControl.grantAccess(user);
                cruiseControl.grantAdminAccess(user);
                break;
        }
    }
}
```

It's easy to fix the unintentional switch fallthrough: make sure that there's a break statement at the end of every case. We've done this in our code example.

Now the code is bug free—but is the switch really the perfect choice here? Nope!

In the example, the switch mixes two different concerns that should be separate: It combines unauthorized access and authorized access into one block of code.

As a rule of thumb, you should put different concerns into different blocks of code (we'll look at that more closely in *Ensure Code Symmetry*, on page 16). First of all, you'll make the code more readable that way. And second, there's a smaller chance of accidental bugs like the switch fallthrough.

You'll find it hard to achieve this separation of concerns with the switch. That's why we prefer using if statements instead. But even there, the switch fallthrough can haunt us, as you'll see in *Always Use Braces*, on page 14.

What if one adds another rank? You would have to adapt this conditional, but that's easy to forget. The code would still run through, and you wouldn't even notice that there's something missing! That's why you should always have a fallback branch that captures values that were not explicitly coded. switch statements have this built in with the default case. Alternatively, you can throw an AssertionError to be sure.

Always Use Braces

```
class BoardComputer {

    CruiseControl cruiseControl;

    void authorize(User user) {
        Objects.requireNonNull(user);
        if (user.isUnknown())
            cruiseControl.logUnauthorizedAccessAttempt();
        if (user.isAstronaut())
            cruiseControl.grantAccess(user);
        if (user.isCommander())
            cruiseControl.grantAccess(user);
            cruiseControl.grantAdminAccess(user);
    }
}
```

Here we've translated the switch statement from the previous comparison into separate if statements. There's one problem, though. The indentation in the snippet is perilously misleading. There are no curly braces after the if, so the condition applies *only* to the subsequent line. That makes the whole method behave maliciously—the line cruiseControl.grantAdminAccess(user); is always executed and grants admin access to any user! What a mess.

The root of this problem isn't the indentation. It's the missing curly braces that define the scoping. Essentially, this is a variant of the switch fallthrough that we've seen in *Avoid Switch Fallthrough*, on page 12.

If you're aware of this problem for a switch, you might still overlook it with an if. Even if you indent correctly, there's no guarantee that anyone would spot the bug during the always hectic crunch times before deadlines. This is why we advise everybody to always use braces.

The Right-Hand Side Is Not Always Meant to Be Perfect

Clean code is hard to achieve. As you might have already noticed, we sometimes iteratively improve the code in the course of two or more comparisons. We aim to improve one thing at a time, sometimes ignoring other code quality criteria to keep the focus on the current topic. Keep this in mind when reading the solutions on the right-hand page. Oftentimes, there's still something more that you can improve.

Take a look at the corrected version.

```
class BoardComputer {

    CruiseControl cruiseControl;

    void authorize(User user) {
        Objects.requireNonNull(user);
        if (user.isUnknown()) {
            cruiseControl.logUnauthorizedAccessAttempt();
        }
        if (user.isAstronaut()) {
            cruiseControl.grantAccess(user);
        }
        if (user.isCommander()) {
            cruiseControl.grantAccess(user);
        }
        cruiseControl.grantAdminAccess(user); // SECURITY THREAT
    }
}
```

Here we've added the curly braces in the way that the compiler treats the code. You can spot the error easily: no condition guards the call of grantAdminAccess(). Thanks to the curly braces, the code is much more readable now. Even if time is short, it's much more likely that someone will spot this critical bug.

It's also safer to add new lines of code now. Before, you might have overlooked the fact that there are no curly braces and added a line into one of the blocks.

Misleading indentation caused the bug in our example. That's dangerous, especially because it was combined with the misplaced thinking that fewer characters mean better code. Remember: Less code is not always better—more readable code is!

You might argue that such an error is unrealistic and would hardly ever happen in practice for security-critical code. History tells otherwise; in 2014, Apple engineers had a very similar bug in the implementation of Apple's SSL/TLS protocol for iOS.[2] Attackers exploiting that bug could eavesdrop to any secure connection of an Apple device. Scary, isn't it?

Always using curly braces out of routine is a good defense against fallthrough bugs, as is always the using auto-indentation of your IDE. But the solution to this problem isn't perfect yet, because it violates *Fail Fast*, on page 74 and *Ensure Code Symmetry*, on page 16. Be sure to read on!

---

2. http://embeddedgurus.com/barr-code/2014/03/apples-gotofail-ssl-security-bug-was-easily-preventable/

Ensure Code Symmetry

```
class BoardComputer {

    CruiseControl cruiseControl;

    void authorize(User user) {
        Objects.requireNonNull(user);
        if (user.isUnknown()) {
            cruiseControl.logUnauthorizedAccessAttempt();
        } else if (user.isAstronaut()) {
            cruiseControl.grantAccess(user);
        } else if (user.isCommander()) {
            cruiseControl.grantAccess(user);
            cruiseControl.grantAdminAccess(user);
        }
    }
}
```

We've emphasized a few times already that understandability is absolutely critical for your code. By structuring your conditional branches in a symmetrical way, you'll make the code easier to understand and easier to grasp. Whoever maintains such code in the future (chances are it'll be you) will be able to locate features more quickly, and it'll be easier to spot bugs.

Here is another modification of the code you have seen in *Avoid Switch Fallthrough*, on page 12 and *Always Use Braces*, on page 14. We've combined the different conditions into a single one with two else if blocks.

There's no outright bug in the code. The problem is that all conditions and statements follow each other subsequently. This requires you to read and understand all of them at once. It might not be too difficult here because it's just a small example without much nesting. But in real life, such structures can grow and become a real puzzle.

In essence, the issue is a lack of *code symmetry*. Check out this definition by Kent Beck[3]: *"Things that are almost the same can be divided into parts that are identical and parts that are clearly different."*

Think about it. Do all branches express a similar concern? Do they show a parallel structure? Or in other words, are all three branches really symmetrical?

The answer is: not really. In the first branch, access is denied. In the second and third branches, access is granted. This isn't symmetrical.

---

3.   https://www.facebook.com/notes/kent-beck/mastering-programming/1184427814923414/

So how would a symmetrical version of this code look?

```
class BoardComputer {

    CruiseControl cruiseControl;

    void authorize(User user) {
        Objects.requireNonNull(user);
        if (user.isUnknown()) {
            cruiseControl.logUnauthorizedAccessAttempt();
            return;
        }

        if (user.isAstronaut()) {
            cruiseControl.grantAccess(user);
        } else if (user.isCommander()) {
            cruiseControl.grantAccess(user);
            cruiseControl.grantAdminAccess(user);
        }
    }
}
```

The asymmetry in the code came from the fact that we were mixing *authorizing* code with *non-authorizing* code. We can improve code symmetry if we separate the two into different blocks of code.

Each part bundles a different type of access with a separate if statement. First, we handle the unauthorized access, log it, and exit the method. Then, we handle the other two cases in an if and a connected else if block.

The second part is symmetrical now, because it contains two types of authorized access. The new structure makes the intent of the condition clearer to the reader. It's also no longer possible to accidentally introduce the fallthrough bug that we've seen in *Avoid Switch Fallthrough*, on page 12.

There's still room for optimization here. For instance, grantAccess() is called in both branches of the second condition with identical arguments. Plus, we could extract the two conditions into separate private methods. This would give us even better signposting in the code.

Note that this points forward to *Fail Fast*, on page 74, as we moved the code for unauthorized access to the top.

What Have You Learned?

So you've read through the first set of comparisons and arrived at this page. First of all, thanks! We're happy that you stuck with us this far. You've already learned a lot about a important topic: writing readable code. Maintaining existing code is what we spend most of our effort on these days, and you'll seldom start a project from the green field. Most of the time, your boss will hurl a gigantic heap of code at you that you're supposed to fix and extend.

When that happens, you'll be grateful if the person who wrote the code cared about readability. So be nice to your fellow programmer and strive for code readability! Also, you never know; even if you think you've concluded a project, your boss might reassign you and then your code comes back to haunt you.

That's why we've shown you how to avoid unnecessary code. You've learned how to simplify Boolean expressions and you'll stay clear of a number of bugs that come from badly readable code, such as the switch fallthrough.

The best thing you can do now is to try out the things you've read about. Take a piece of code you wrote a while ago and take a look at it. Can you apply some of the recommendations you've read about here? How does your code look after these refactorings? Be sure to keep a copy of the original version to compare it against the improved one. After all, that's the theme of this book!

When you're ready, turn to the next chapter. We'll dig deeper into the topic of code readability and understandability with some more advanced recommendations on code style and the use of the Java API. So be sure to read on!

Good code is short, simple, and symmetrical—the challenge is figuring out how to get there.

        Sean Parent

CHAPTER 2

Level Up Your Code Style

In role-playing games, no matter whether they're digital or tabletop, you usually play a character with a unique set of skills. As the game progresses, your character moves through the game world, interacts with its inhabitants, and gathers experience through quests. Eventually, your character will gain new skills and "level up" her skills to a new a stage of mastery, becoming faster, stronger, smarter, or whatever it was you were practicing.

Programming is similar to playing games, and it can be just as addictive. It's real life, so you don't control a character—you *are* in the game. You move through the digital world and gather experience. You discover distant places of programming languages with very different language paradigms. You meet fellow programmers who have different viewpoints on the most intricate aspects of style, such as whether to put a curly bracket in a new line. You practice your skills by programming, learning new frameworks or language concepts that you were unaware of, and sharpening your understanding of the ones you already know. Eventually, you rise to a new level of proficiency in programming.

This chapter is a level up from the more basic items we discussed in the previous chapter. We'll go through a number of more advanced concepts of the Java language, as well as aspects of code style.

You'll learn how to deal with magic numbers—either by replacing them with constants or, even better, with enums—and you'll see why it makes sense to use newlines for grouping code. On top of that, we'll show you why you should rely on the Java API as often as possible, and we'll go over several typical pitfalls you should avoid when you do so. You'll see how to best iterate over data structures without triggering unwanted exceptions or causing performance problems. Lastly, we'll provide you with a handy method for formatting strings in your code. So let's get to the next level!

Replace Magic Numbers with Constants

```
class CruiseControl {

    private double targetSpeedKmh;

    void setPreset(int speedPreset) {
        if (speedPreset == 2) {
            setTargetSpeedKmh(16944);
        } else if (speedPreset == 1) {
            setTargetSpeedKmh(7667);
        } else if (speedPreset == 0) {
            setTargetSpeedKmh(0);
        }
    }

    void setTargetSpeedKmh(double speed) {
        targetSpeedKmh = speed;
    }
}
```

Oftentimes when programmers need to represent a set of options in code, they use a set of numbers. Without additional context, we call those numbers *"magic numbers"*: numbers without an apparent meaning that steer the program. They make your code harder to understand and more error-prone.

This code snippet depicts a cruise control. It lets you set a targetSpeedKmh by calling setPreset() with an integer that the CruiseControl translates into a concrete value.

The current solution is very prone to errors and easy to misuse. If you call setPreset(), you need to have in-depth knowledge of the internals of the method. Otherwise, you can't select a proper speedPreset as input.

Also, the actual targetSpeedKmh that a speedPreset corresponds to is arbitrary. Since the CruiseControl communicates no information of available speed presets, you have to know the options by heart.

Obviously, code that uses magic numbers is harder to understand. It's also easy to misuse. The compiler won't prevent you from entering a number that the code doesn't know.

Let's see how we can improve the code and dispel the magic in these numbers.

```java
class CruiseControl {
    static final int STOP_PRESET = 0;
    static final int PLANETARY_SPEED_PRESET = 1;
    static final int CRUISE_SPEED_PRESET = 2;

    static final double CRUISE_SPEED_KMH = 16944;
    static final double PLANETARY_SPEED_KMH = 7667;
    static final double STOP_SPEED_KMH = 0;

    private double targetSpeedKmh;

    void setPreset(int speedPreset) {
        if (speedPreset == CRUISE_SPEED_PRESET) {
            setTargetSpeedKmh(CRUISE_SPEED_KMH);
        } else if (speedPreset == PLANETARY_SPEED_PRESET) {
            setTargetSpeedKmh(PLANETARY_SPEED_KMH);
        } else if (speedPreset == STOP_PRESET) {
            setTargetSpeedKmh(STOP_SPEED_KMH);
        }
    }

    void setTargetSpeedKmh(double speed) {
        targetSpeedKmh = speed;
    }
}
```

This time, we got rid of the *magic* part. We've done this by assigning each number a meaningful and accessible name.

In this code, we've added variables for all available preset options and target speeds. These variables are static and final—that is, they're *constants*. The modifiers make sure that the variables exist once and only once (static) and that they can't be changed (final). We've written the names of the constants in all caps, which is a Java code convention.

Arguably, the static modifier is an optimization. We might have valid reasons to tie the variables to instances of CruiseControl after all. In any case, you should make the variables final. Otherwise they'd be mutable and could be changed at any point in time.

Based on the variable names, it's now much clearer which speed presets and target speeds exist. But we can do even better! Take a look at *Favor Enums Over Integer Constants*, on page 22.

Favor Enums Over Integer Constants

```java
class CruiseControl {
    static final int STOP_PRESET = 0;
    static final int PLANETARY_SPEED_PRESET = 1;
    static final int CRUISE_SPEED_PRESET = 2;

    static final double STOP_SPEED_KMH = 0;
    static final double PLANETARY_SPEED_KMH = 7667;
    static final double CRUISE_SPEED_KMH = 16944;

    private double targetSpeedKmh;

    void setPreset(int speedPreset) {
        if (speedPreset == CRUISE_SPEED_PRESET) {
            setTargetSpeedKmh(CRUISE_SPEED_KMH);
        } else if (speedPreset == PLANETARY_SPEED_PRESET) {
            setTargetSpeedKmh(PLANETARY_SPEED_KMH);
        } else if (speedPreset == STOP_PRESET) {
            setTargetSpeedKmh(STOP_SPEED_KMH);
        }
    }

    void setTargetSpeedKmh(double speedKmh) {
        targetSpeedKmh = speedKmh;
    }
}
```

Constants, as you've seen them in the previous comparison, *Replace Magic Numbers with Constants*, on page 20, are a big improvement over magic numbers. But in case you can enumerate all options, Java's type system offers an even better solution.

In this code, the input parameter speedPreset is still an integer. That means it's still possible to put any integer value, even a negative one, into setPreset(). No one forces you to actually use the constants, such as STOP_PRESET, after all.

If you put an invalid integer value into setPreset(), the method does more or less nothing. It checks the conditions, and then returns without altering the state or throwing an error. That's better than crashing, but it can still lead to all kinds of bugs in your program.

In statically typed languages like Java, there are features that you should use to spot such errors as early as possible, even before the program is executed the first time. The earlier you spot an error, the cheaper it is to fix it!

So how can we transform this to ensure that the compiler rejects illegal values?

```java
class CruiseControl {

    private double targetSpeedKmh;

    void setPreset(SpeedPreset speedPreset) {
        Objects.requireNonNull(speedPreset);

        setTargetSpeedKmh(speedPreset.speedKmh);
    }

    void setTargetSpeedKmh(double speedKmh) {
        targetSpeedKmh = speedKmh;
    }
}
enum SpeedPreset {
    STOP(0), PLANETARY_SPEED(7667), CRUISE_SPEED(16944);

    final double speedKmh;

    SpeedPreset(double speedKmh) {
        this.speedKmh = speedKmh;
    }
}
```

Java's type system can be a big help in preventing illegal input values on occasions like this. If you can enumerate all available options, such as in this example, it's always preferable to use an enum type instead of an integer.

In the solution, we created a new enum named SpeedPreset with a single variable that captures the speedKmh for a given instance. This enum enumerates all available options: STOP, PLANETARY_SPEED, and CRUISE_SPEED.

The key advantage here is that you can no longer put a nonexistent SpeedPreset into the setPreset() method. Even if you try, the Java compiler will stop you.

We're also still referencing speaking names instead of bare numbers, as in *Replace Magic Numbers with Constants*, on page 20. On top of that, we got rid of the constants for the actual targetSpeedKmh, because they're already part of the enum.

Finally, we could even remove the if-elseif-block in setPreset(). Now, the code is less complex and looks much more concise.

Favor For-Each Over For Loops

```
class LaunchChecklist {

    List<String> checks = Arrays.asList("Cabin Pressure",
                                        "Communication",
                                        "Engine");

    Status prepareForTakeoff(Commander commander) {
        for (int i = 0; i < checks.size(); i++) {
            boolean shouldAbortTakeoff = commander.isFailing(checks.get(i));
            if (shouldAbortTakeoff) {
                return Status.ABORT_TAKE_OFF;
            }
        }
        return Status.READY_FOR_TAKE_OFF;
    }
}
```

There are many ways to iterate over a data structure. The one that beginners are usually taught isn't exactly the best one.

The code here shows an iteration on a data structure, a List named checks. It uses a for loop and iterates over checks using an index variable i.

This is a very traditional way of iterating, available in all C-style programming languages. It's often associated with arrays, but in Java, it works with all kinds of indexed collections (but doesn't work for Set or Map). It has the advantage that you always have the current iteration index, i, at hand.

But in this snippet, we don't use the index except for accessing the next element of the list. So why should we keep track of it?

What's more, the index variable opens the door to mistakes. It's not protected, and you can overwrite it at any time. Getting the termination criterion right is something that beginners notoriously struggle with. This can result in embarrassing IndexOutOfBoundsExceptions.

Most of the time, you don't really need the level of detail that an index variable gives you. In those cases, you should write loops in a different way, such that the low-level details of the iteration aren't just protected but are also hidden from the programmer.

This makes your software safer and easier to understand!

Luckily, Java offers several alternative syntaxes for this. As a rule of thumb, you should use the easiest one available.

```java
class LaunchChecklist {

    List<String> checks = Arrays.asList("Cabin Pressure",
                                        "Communication",
                                        "Engine");

    Status prepareForTakeoff(Commander commander) {
        for (String check : checks) {
            boolean shouldAbortTakeoff = commander.isFailing(check);
            if (shouldAbortTakeoff) {
                return Status.ABORT_TAKE_OFF;
            }
        }
        return Status.READY_FOR_TAKE_OFF;
    }
}
```

This syntax looks a bit odd first, but proves to be really convenient. Read it as *"for each check in checks do the following..."* It defines a local variable that we can use to access an item of the collection—String check, in our example—followed by a colon and the data structure that's iterated upon—checks.

On every iteration, Java makes sure that a new object from the data structure is assigned to check. No need to handle an iteration index anymore! And it even works for arrays and unindexed collections like Set.

In most cases, this is the syntax you should go with. It's obvious that each element of the collection is processed, and this syntax protects the state of the iteration (the index i from the problem) against manipulation. Note that there's a naming convention to use for(Type singular : plural) as variable names.

Another alternative looping mechanism is using an iterator like in *Avoid Collection Modification During Iteration*, on page 26.

You might ask yourself when it's more appropriate to use the traditional way of iterating with an index. The answer is: almost never. Most of the time, you just want to process every element of a data structure.

If this is the case, then dealing with indices is an implementation detail you shouldn't have to worry about. The rare cases where index-based iteration makes sense is when you only iterate over special parts of collections or you explicitly need the index for other purposes.

Avoid Collection Modification During Iteration

```java
class Inventory {

    private List<Supply> supplies = new ArrayList<>();

    void disposeContaminatedSupplies() {
        for (Supply supply : supplies) {
            if (supply.isContaminated()) {
                supplies.remove(supply);
            }
        }
    }
}
```

We iterate over arrays, lists, or other data structures all the time. Most of the time, we only read from those data structures—for instance, when creating an invoice from a list of ordered items or searching for an item in a list by name. But you need to be careful when you modify the structure. Otherwise, you risk crashing your program.

This code describes a fairly simple iteration over a data structure: a List of supplies. If a Supply isContaminated(), the inventory system removes it from the List.

This code looks completely innocent, doesn't it?

Although the code looks okay, it'll crash reliably when at least one Supply in the inventory list is contaminated. Even worse, it'll work fine until this happens the first time. And worse yet, it'll work fine if all supplies are clean, making the bug hard to detect.

The problem is that we call supplies.remove(supply) while we're inside a for loop that iterates over the supplies. In this situation, a standard implementation of the List interface, or indeed of other Collection interfaces such as Set or Queue, will throw a ConcurrentModificationException. We can't simply modify a List while we iterate over it.

The name ConcurrentModificationException makes many people wonder about concurrency in their single-threaded application. That's quite misleading, since no actual concurrency takes place here! Instead, we *iterate* over the Collection, and while we're doing that, we *modify* that collection. Unfortunately, no compile-time check in Java saves us from this error.

So how can you do this properly without raising the ConcurrentModificationException?

```java
class Inventory {

    private List<Supply> supplies = new ArrayList<>();

    void disposeContaminatedSupplies() {
        Iterator<Supply> iterator = supplies.iterator();
        while (iterator.hasNext()) {
            if (iterator.next().isContaminated()) {
                iterator.remove();
            }
        }
    }
}
```

In the straightforward solution to this problem, we would iterate the list in search of any contaminated supplies, and *afterward*, we would remove any previously found supplies. Think of a two-step approach: first iterate and then modify.

This would work, but it would require quite a few lines of code. And we would need to save the contaminated supplies in a temporary data structure during iteration. This would consume extra time and memory.

The solution we've depicted here uses another way of iteration: a while loop that relies on the Iterator of our supplies collection. The Iterator is our rescue. It acts like a pointer to an element in the list, starting with the first one. We can ask if any elements are left via hasNext(), get the next() element, and safely remove() the last element returned.

Although we can't modify a List directly, the iterator is perfectly capable of doing this. Its job is to make sure that everything works during the iteration.

Technically, the for-each loop in the previous example also builds on such an iterator, but it hides this fact from the programmer. That's nice, since it reduces the complexity of the code. But it also prevents us from using the remove() method of the iterator itself.

Some special List implementations like the CopyOnWriteArrayList can deal with modification during iteration. But such characteristics come at a price. Do you really want to copy the *whole* list each time you add or remove an element of it? Since Java 8, you can also use the new Collection.removeIf() method that makes use of lambdas. But be sure to read Chapter 8, *Let Your Data Flow*, on page 129 before you use that method!

Avoid Compute-Intense Operations During Iteration

```java
class Inventory {

    private List<Supply> supplies = new ArrayList<>();

    List<Supply> find(String regex) {
        List<Supply> result = new LinkedList<>();
        for (Supply supply : supplies) {
            if (Pattern.matches(regex, supply.toString())) {
                result.add(supply);
            }
        }
        return result;
    }
}
```

When you iterate over a data structure, you need to be careful with what kind of operations you perform. If you do something that is compute-intense, it can easily turn into a performance pitfall. The code above shows a typical example for this with the method find() that locates Supply objects with a regular expression.

In Java, or in any other programming language, you'll build query strings using a regular expression—*regex* for short. A regex enables efficient queries on large sets of textual data.

To get familiar with regexes, we recommend you look at java.util.regex.Pattern[1] in the Java API. This class is Java's representation of regular expressions, and it offers a variety of methods for building and executing them. The most straightforward way is probably the one you see in the code snippet above: you just call the static method matches() and provide it with a regex String and a String to search in. This is handy, but it's a performance pitfall. During execution, Java takes the expression String, regex, and constructs a special-purpose automaton from it. This automaton will accept Strings that follow the pattern, rejecting all others.

In Pattern.matches(regex, supply.toString()) we both compile such an automaton and try to match supply.toString() to it. Compiling a regex automaton consumes time and processing power, just as the compilation of a class takes time. Usually, it's a one-time effort, but here the regex is compiled *on every iteration*.

Be aware that some other very popular methods in the Java API, such as String.replaceAll(), behave the same way!

---

1. https://docs.oracle.com/javase/9/docs/api/java/util/regex/Pattern.html

So how can you prevent the compilation of a single regular expression over and over?

```java
class Inventory {

    private List<Supply> supplies = new ArrayList<>();

    List<Supply> find(String regex) {
        List<Supply> result = new LinkedList<>();
        Pattern pattern = Pattern.compile(regex);
        for (Supply supply : supplies) {
            if (pattern.matcher(supply.toString()).matches()) {
                result.add(supply);
            }
        }
        return result;
    }
}
```

The solution to the potential performance pitfall is very simple: make sure that the computation-intense operation takes place as rarely as possible.

Here, you should only compile the regex once for every method call. After all, the expression string doesn't change between each iteration of the loop.

Luckily, we can get a single compilation easily with the Pattern API. To do so, we need to separate the two operations that are bundled in the call of Pattern.matches(). First, this is the compilation of the expression and, second, its execution on the search string.

We can extract the first step through a call to Pattern.compile(), which creates a compiled regular expression, an instance of Pattern. This is the computation-intense step, and we can store its result in a local variable.

The second step, the execution of the compiled expression, is the easy and quick one. It's also the one that we need to execute for every instance of Supply, so it needs to go into the body of the loop.

Here, we first create a Matcher for the String we want to search. This is a handle for searching in different fashions, even iteratively. In this case, we need to check only if a supply matches the regular expression at all, which we can do by calling matches().

To sum up, with regexes, a little modification can mean a big difference in performance!

Group with New Lines

```
enum DistanceUnit {

    MILES, KILOMETERS;

    static final double MILE_IN_KILOMETERS = 1.60934;
    static final int IDENTITY = 1;
    static final double KILOMETER_IN_MILES = 1 / MILE_IN_KILOMETERS;

    double getConversionRate(DistanceUnit unit) {
        if (this == unit) {
            return IDENTITY;
        }
        if (this == MILES && unit == KILOMETERS) {
            return MILE_IN_KILOMETERS;
        } else {
            return KILOMETER_IN_MILES;
        }
    }
}
```

If blocks of code are pressed next to each other, you get the impression that they belong together. You can improve the readability of your code a lot if you separate distinct blocks with new lines.

The code here shows an enum that returns the conversion rate between miles and kilometers. Actually, the semantics of that code are fine[2] and the problem is quite concealed. We've already applied *Replace Magic Numbers with Constants*, on page 20, so what could be wrong?

Simple: What's missing is space! In particular, getConversionRate() glues all lines of code together. But is this really a single block or does it consist of different parts? We can improve the readability of the code by adding empty lines that act as a separator. It's similar to this book, which captures single thoughts or arguments within paragraphs separated by new lines.

We've already separated the enum values from the constants through an empty line. But take a look at the two highlighted lines of code. Does this seem right to you?

---

2. Admittedly, the code is somewhat brittle. You can't easily add a conversion to a third unit without rewriting the method. This comparison is about formatting not extensibility, so we'll ignore that problem for now.

That leads to the question: where would an empty line make sense? Which parts should be separated? Which parts should be kept together?

```java
enum DistanceUnit {

    MILES, KILOMETERS;

    static final int IDENTITY = 1;

    static final double MILE_IN_KILOMETERS = 1.60934;
    static final double KILOMETER_IN_MILES = 1 / MILE_IN_KILOMETERS;

    double getConversionRate(DistanceUnit unit) {
        if (this == unit) {
            return IDENTITY;
        }

        if (this == MILES && unit == KILOMETERS) {
            return MILE_IN_KILOMETERS;
        } else {
            return KILOMETER_IN_MILES;
        }
    }
}
```

In our solution, we've separated some parts of the code by new lines.

First, we've separated the IDENTITY field from the other constants. This field should stand alone, because it's independent of a particular unit and more abstract than the two conversion rates between miles and kilometers.

In getConversionRate(), we've separated the two if statements from each other. We've done this because they check for different things: the first one performs an identity check, the second one a conversion. An empty line makes that more obvious to the reader through a vertical separation.

As a rule of thumb, you should try to group related code and concepts together and separate different groups from each other through empty lines.

The concept of vertical space goes even further. Robert C. Martin uses the metaphor of a newspaper in his book *Clean Code [Mar08]* for describing vertical formatting. A good article starts with the title (class name), goes over section headings (public members, constructors, and methods), down to its very details (private methods). If you structure your code this way, you'll find it much easier to make sense of a class already if you only scroll over the code. Chances are, it's easier to locate features in the class as well.

Favor Format Over Concatenation

```java
class Mission {

    Logbook logbook;
    LocalDate start;

    void update(String author, String message) {
        LocalDate today = LocalDate.now();
        String month = String.valueOf(today.getMonthValue());
        String formattedMonth = month.length() < 2 ? "0" + month : month;
        String entry = author.toUpperCase() + ": [" + formattedMonth + "-" +
                today.getDayOfMonth() + "-" + today.getYear() + "](Day " +
                (ChronoUnit.DAYS.between(start, today) + 1) + ")> " +
                message + System.lineSeparator();
        logbook.write(entry);
    }
}
```

Understandability and readability don't just matter in your code—they're also important for the output your code produces.

If you have to build large strings, you can use format strings to make them more readable.

Here, we're revisiting the log book we already mentioned in *Avoid NullPointerException in Conditionals*, on page 10. The problem is that it's quite hard to see what the output will actually look like. There are multiple String variables, some of them using Java's in-line notation.

The code isn't really complex. There's no deep nesting, no conditional branching, and even the names of variables and methods are meaningful. Despite all this, it's comparably hard to read. The number of plusses, quotes, and spaces obfuscates the actual processing going on (humans are generally better at understanding words in a natural language than combinations of symbols). This makes the code harder to read and increases the chance of making mistakes when writing it.

Additionally, performing in-line computations like summing int values adds to the confusion, as the + operator has different semantics when it comes to Strings and ints. Using it with different semantics in the very same line makes it even harder to maintain an overview of what's happening. Don't do this!

We can trim this down a lot. Take a look at the following code:

```
class Mission {

    Logbook logbook;
    LocalDate start;

    void update(String author, String message) {
        final LocalDate today = LocalDate.now();
        String entry = String.format("%S: [%tm-%<te-%<tY](Day %d)> %s%n",
                author, today,
                ChronoUnit.DAYS.between(start, today) + 1, message);
        logbook.write(entry);
    }
}
```

Format strings help to overcome this issue, and they're available in practically any contemporary programming language—not just in Java. The key lies in separating the layout of a String (*how* it is printed) from the data (*what* is being printed). Format strings define a coherent String in a single block using special placeholder characters, marked by %.

Format methods, such as String.format(), or System.out.printf(), accept data using placeholder characters in the order in which they're listed after the String.

In our example here, %S converts an object into an upper case String using its toString() method. The parameter author will be processed this way. The date variable today serves as data for %tm, the month, %te the day of the month, and %tY, the year. The additional character < makes sure that all three placeholders read the same input data. %d processes a decimal value and %s accepts a String. Finally, %n is the symbol for a line break.

The actual data is listed in a nicely formatted fashion after the String layout. This makes it a little more acceptable to perform in-line computations, as we can use one line for each parameter. Point taken that it's not so easy to see what "%S: [%tm-%<te-%<tY](Day %d)> %s%n" will print in the end. But it's a well-documented standard[3] and actually a good alternative to the cluttered code from the problem—for large strings we recommend StringTemplate,[4] a powerful template engine.

Consider documenting the formatted string with a few examples similar to *Document Using Examples*, on page 48 so that the next developer reading your code doesn't have to look up how %S or any other special formatting syntax behaves to know what the resulting string will be.

---

3. https://docs.oracle.com/javase/9/docs/api/java/util/Formatter.html
4. http://www.stringtemplate.org/

Favor Java API Over DIY

```java
class Inventory {

    private List<Supply> supplies = new ArrayList<>();

    int getQuantity(Supply supply) {
        if (supply == null) {
            throw new NullPointerException("supply must not be null");
        }

        int quantity = 0;
        for (Supply supplyInStock : supplies) {
            if (supply.equals(supplyInStock)) {
                quantity++;
            }
        }

        return quantity;
    }
}
```

In the early days of programming, you had to do everything by yourself. In C, for instance, you still need to create a String using a char[] or implement your own list. You had to do this for all kinds of data structures and algorithms. Although this is a nice exercise, it's also time-consuming and error-prone.

Times have changed. The Java API is huge, and it comes with many classes that can help you get the job done, such as String or List. Instead of reimplementing functionality from the API, you should reuse it whenever possible. Experts have written and optimized the Java API over time, resulting in a fast and practically bug-free standard library.

You already know the inventory system from *Avoid Collection Modification During Iteration*, on page 26 and other comparisons. Above, you can see the getQuantity() method, which informs us about the quantity of a Supply in stock.

At a first glance, the code looks good. The method validates its input parameter to avoid null values. It uses an abstract type for its internal data structure, as we recommend in *Favor Abstract Over Concrete Types*, on page 118. It also iterates over the data structure with a for-each loop instead of a regular for loop, as we recommend in *Favor For-Each Over For Loops*, on page 24.

We can vastly improve this code—it's much more verbose than it needs to be.

```java
class Inventory {

    private List<Supply> supplies = new ArrayList<>();

    int getQuantity(Supply supply) {
        Objects.requireNonNull(supply, "supply must not be null");

        return Collections.frequency(supplies, supply);
    }
}
```

Now that's much shorter! This version yields the same result, but it uses the functionality of the Java API instead of custom code. Now that it's shorter, it's much more readable and easier to understand.

The utility class Collections provides a frequency() method that counts the number of occurrences of objects in a Collection. Plus, we have used the method requireNonNull() from the utility class Objects you've seen before, for example in *Avoid Switch Fallthrough*, on page 12. This method throws a NullPointerException with a message if an object is null. With these methods, we're able to condense twelve lines of code into a single return statement!

The Java class library, the Java API for short, is huge. It contains thousands of classes with all sorts of useful functionality that's available to you at any given point in your code. It also offers several utility classes, which you can usually spot by an appended s, such as the Collections class for Collection-related helper methods or Objects for general-purpose operations on Objects.

You can often solve problems in your code much more concisely if you know the API. And just as important, the API received and receives extensive testing worldwide, which is probably more than you can do. Chances are that your code is more prone to bugs than the API.

Knowing the API well is what makes a true Java professional. You save time if you don't reimplement (and test) functionality that's already there.

There is a lot more functionality beyond what we have shown here—such as the conversion of time values with TimeUnit. We encourage you to explore the Java API!

What Have You Learned?

You've already finished one more chapter. Welcome to the next level!

Now you know how to deal with magic numbers, and you can replace them with constants or enums as the situation requires. You're able to implement iteration in the way that best fits your needs, and you'll stay clear of exceptions or performance pitfalls while you're at it. You know how to format your code in a readable way, and you've seen how the Java API can help you to make it more concise and efficient.

That last part's important, and the learning doesn't stop here. The Java API is huge—*really* huge. In Java 9, there are more than 4,000 public API classes alone. Each one of these has a purpose that can help you. We don't recommend that you go through all of them right now. But when you're programming, ask yourself now and then, "Could this piece of code be useful in a different context as well?" If the answer is yes, then there's a chance that you can find a helpful class in the Java API. So you should try searching the API at least briefly.

Eventually, you'll learn about other helpful classes, similar to Collections or Objects. And you'll get more and more proficient in using them over time. In the end, knowing your API is what makes a true professional.

In the next chapter, we'll get more specific and zoom in on one particular aspect of programming: code comments. They don't influence the execution of your code, which is why many programmers don't pay them much respect. But good comments can mean a huge difference to the readability of your code. As we've mentioned now and then (read: all of the time), that's really important. So make sure that you can apply comments in the right way!

CHAPTER 3

Use Comments Wisely

One of us (Jörg) recently bought a new TV—a smart TV with all kinds of apps, streaming services, and different ways to program a time-based video recording. Turns out, this smart TV is only as smart as the person using it, and learning how to get all the new features to work isn't all that straightforward. You'd have better luck teaching yourself a few new swear words than finding the folder where the TV stores a new recording. And why doesn't it warn you that it's going to stop recording if you hit the Power button?

That's when most people pick up the user manual. The manual is the documentation—it's there to help you with clarification. It should tell you things like where you can find your recordings and how to record something without watching it at the same time. But with this smart TV, picking up the manual only caused more frustration. In the section titled "The Record Button," all it says is, "Starts the recording." Anyone could figure that much out just by looking at the red Record button! And what happens if you hit the Power button during recording? It doesn't say.

User manuals are meant to tell you how something works. Same thing with comments in your code: their purpose is to tell you how a piece of code works. Unfortunately, code comments are often like our smart TV's manual—not helpful. For example, maybe they just repeat what's already in the code. Or worse—they'll tell a different story than the actual code.

In this chapter, you're going to learn how to make your comments more helpful. In the pages that follow, we'll help you sharpen your senses for when to use comments and when to avoid them. We'll show you types of comments that are simply superfluous, tell you what to do with code that's been commented out, and introduce you to a few tricks you can use to replace a comment with code. Finally, we'll explore the commenting conventions in Java so you'll be able to write high-quality JavaDoc comments. Let's get started.

Remove Superfluous Comments

```java
class Inventory {
    // Fields (we only have one)
    List<Supply> supplies = new ArrayList<>(); // The list of supplies.

    // Methods
    int countContaminatedSupplies() {
        // TODO: check if field is already initialized (not null)

        int contaminatedCounter = 0; // the counter
        // No supplies => no contamination
        for (Supply supply : supplies) { // begin FOR
            if (supply.isContaminated()) {
                contaminatedCounter++; // increment counter!
            } // End IF supply is contaminated
        }// End FOR

        // Returns the number of contaminated supplies.
        return contaminatedCounter; // Handle with care!
    }
} // End of Inventory class
```

You've probably heard that comments are very important. They are, of course, but only if they add important information (the *why*). If they don't, then they're just getting in the way.

The code above shows the Inventory class that you have seen in a few comparisons before. As you can see by the amount of green text, it contains *a lot* of comments.

If you just skim the code, you might think that it's very well documented. And code quality tools will mark this code as "good" in terms of commenting. But that's just not true.

Most of these comments are superfluous because they only repeat what the code says. Two comments state Fields or Methods, but this is already clear from Java's syntax. Several other comments are meant to mark the ending of code blocks, such as End IF, End FOR, or End of Inventory class. This is already clear from the indentation.

The most critical comment is probably this one: TODO: check if field is already initialized (not null). Here, the comment really deviates from the code, so this indicates an actual problem.

We can make this a lot more concise! Consider this:

```java
class Inventory {

    List<Supply> supplies = new ArrayList<>();

    int countContaminatedSupplies() {
        if (supplies == null || supplies.isEmpty()) {
            // No supplies => no contamination
            return 0;
        }

        int contaminatedCounter = 0;
        for (Supply supply : supplies) {
            if (supply.isContaminated()) {
                contaminatedCounter++;
            }
        }

        return contaminatedCounter;
    }
}
```

We've changed the code very little here, but there's hardly any green text left.

First of all, we've deleted all comments that just state what you can already read straight-out from a line of code. All comments that mark the end of a code block (End IF, End FOR, etc.) are gone. The indentation tells us that already, but you'll be surprised how often you find these comments not only in legacy code, but also in well-known libraries.

We've done the same with all comments that highlight the class structure (Fields, Methods, Returns). If you follow the class structure that the Java code conventions set out, then there's no need for this sort of signposting.

Next, we've deleted all comments that just rephrase the code, such as contaminatedCounter++; // increment counter. If a comment doesn't add anything on top of the code, there's no point in having it.

We've also fixed the TODO comment and added a null and isEmpty() check instead. If you can't fix a TODO, create an issue in your issue tracker instead where you can discuss and track that problem until it's fixed.

The only comment we've kept is the one that adds information that isn't obvious from the code. In case the supplies are null or empty, we've chosen a graceful continuation by returning zero. We could've thrown an exception instead, so there is a reason for including the comment. You could say that it documents a design decision.

Remove Commented-Out Code

```
class LaunchChecklist {

    List<String> checks = Arrays.asList(
            "Cabin Leak",
            // "Communication", // Do we actually want to talk to Houston?
            "Engine",
            "Hull",
            // "Rover", // We won't need it, I think...
            "OxygenTank"
            //"Supplies"
    );

    Status prepareLaunch(Commander commander) {
        for (String check : checks) {
            boolean shouldAbortTakeoff = commander.isFailing(check);
            if (shouldAbortTakeoff) {
                //System.out.println("REASON FOR ABORT: " + item);
                return Status.ABORT_TAKE_OFF;
            }
        }
        return Status.READY_FOR_TAKE_OFF;
    }
}
```

In any bigger code base, you're guaranteed to find sections of commented-out code. These types of comments are just clutter.

In this example, you see the LaunchChecklist we've visited in *Favor For-Each Over For Loops*, on page 24. Several list items are commented out. Even the comments attached to these items are commented. That's a little too much for our taste.

Apart from the list items, the method prepareLaunch() includes a commented-out print statement. If you look closely, you'll notice that the print statement accesses the undeclared variable item—preventing you from simply uncommenting it.

Commented-out code is a huge problem. Unlike normal comments, they aren't meant to clarify anything. Instead, they add clutter to the code that can only increase confusion.

Programmers usually comment out code because it prevents them from getting a feature to work. They're focused on other aspects, and commenting gives them an easy way out. Some are also afraid of losing code they might need again in the future and prefer to comment it instead.

You might not be surprised by the solution:

```
class LaunchChecklist {

    List<String> checks = Arrays.asList(
            "Cabin Leak",
            "Engine",
            "Hull",
            "OxygenTank"
    );

    Status prepareLaunch(Commander commander) {
        for (String check : checks) {
            boolean shouldAbortTakeoff = commander.isFailing(check);
            if (shouldAbortTakeoff) {
                return Status.ABORT_TAKE_OFF;
            }
        }
        return Status.READY_FOR_TAKE_OFF;
    }
}
```

Fortunately, commented-out code is very easy to deal with: just remove it.

Commented-out code always decreases the understandability. It doesn't add any new information. It just adds lines of text—lines that are never executed. Some programmers are also afraid of changing classes that contain commented-out code because they don't know if their changes break the relation between the actual code and the comments.

Today, virtually every professional project is hosted on a version control system. This system tracks every change in the code, including code removal. You can easily inspect changes and go back in time if you're looking for certain parts of code. In our projects, we literally *never* experienced a situation where a developer wanted to uncomment commented-out code. Instead, they all tried to remove it.

To sum up, it's really a no-brainer to remove commented-out code—it's only harmful to understandability, and you can't actually lose it when you use a version control system (although you probably won't try to find that commented-out code again).

Version Control Systems

Although there are many version control systems, nowadays you will probably need only one: Git. It's blazing fast and you can get free public and sometimes even free private repositories from many providers such as github.com, gitlab.com, or bitbucket.org.

Replace Comments with Constants

```
enum SmallDistanceUnit {

    CENTIMETER,
    INCH;

    double getConversionRate(SmallDistanceUnit unit) {
        if (this == unit) {
            return 1; // identity conversion rate
        }

        if (this == CENTIMETER && unit == INCH) {
            return 0.393701; // one centimeter in inch
        } else {
            return 2.54; // one inch in centimeters
        }
    }
}
```

Comments are there to explain the code. But it's even better if the code speaks for itself!

In this example, you see a unit conversion. It's very similar to what you've seen in *Group with New Lines*, on page 30, just for small instead of large distances. The method getConversionRate() returns a conversion rate number. For each number, there's a comment that explains what the number is supposed to mean. The first one's the identity conversion, and the other two convert from centimeters to inches and the other way around.

Without the comments, the numbers would be *magic numbers*, which you've seen in *Replace Magic Numbers with Constants*, on page 20. Here, the comments take out the "magic" and give a meaning to the numbers.

That's a good start. After all, it's clearly beneficial that the comments are there. But there's a way we can make the code more meaningful on its own.

Consider the solution here:

```
enum SmallDistanceUnit {

    CENTIMETER,
    INCH;

    static final double INCH_IN_CENTIMETERS = 2.54;
    static final double CENTIMETER_IN_INCHES = 1 / INCH_IN_CENTIMETERS;
    static final int IDENTITY = 1;

    double getConversionRate(SmallDistanceUnit unit) {
        if (this == unit) {
            return IDENTITY;
        }

        if (this == CENTIMETER && unit == INCH) {
            return CENTIMETER_IN_INCHES;
        } else {
            return INCH_IN_CENTIMETERS;
        }
    }
}
```

We've basically applied *Replace Magic Numbers with Constants*, on page 20 here. While we did so, we removed the comments and merged them into the names of the constants. So in a way, we've "embedded" the comments into the code.

The code is much more self-explanatory. There's more of it now since we've added several constants. The benefit of these constants is that they explain their meaning in their names. That's why there's no longer any need for additional explanation with comments: the comments have turned into actual code.

Comments always have a risk of becoming stale. Programmers rarely apply the same rigor to comments as they do to code. Someone might change the code but ignore the comment, or they might add a new conversion rate without documenting it.

If you capture the explanation of the code in things like naming, then it's less likely that people will ignore it when they change code. As a rule of thumb, whenever you can merge a comment into the name of a constant, variable, field, or method, go for it!

Replace Comments with Utility Methods

```
class FuelSystem {

    List<Double> tanks = new ArrayList<>();

    int getAverageTankFillingPercent() {
        double sum = 0;
        for (double tankFilling : tanks) {
            sum += tankFilling;
        }
        double averageFuel = sum / tanks.size();
        // round to integer percent
        return Math.toIntExact(Math.round(averageFuel * 100));
    }
}
```

Converting comments into constants is one tool that's available to you. But what if things are more complicated? After all, not everything's a fixed value.

Here you can see code that calculates an average and manipulates its value before returning it. Can you immediately spot what the last statement is supposed to do? We'd say that the author was absolutely right to clarify the final line with a comment.

From the previous pages, you can probably already guess that we don't like the comment. But what to do about it?

One alternative would be to create a named variable like this:

```
int roundedToPercent = Math.toIntExact(Math.round(averageFuel * 100));
return roundedToPercent;
```

This clarifies the code and gets rid of the comment. But it adds another variable to the method, and that one is pretty redundant. After all, it's returned right away.

Let's see if we can do better!

The right way to go here is to introduce a utility method. Take a look:

```
class FuelSystem {

    List<Double> tanks = new ArrayList<>();

    int getAverageTankFillingPercent() {
        double sum = 0;
        for (double tankFilling : tanks) {
            sum += tankFilling;
        }
        double averageFuel = sum / tanks.size();
        return roundToIntegerPercent(averageFuel);
    }

    static int roundToIntegerPercent(double value) {
        return Math.toIntExact(Math.round(value * 100));
    }
}
```

You get several advantages from a utility method compared to a comment or an additional variable.

First, the method gets rid of the comment because it says in its name what the code does. That's also what you would get from a variable. But there are even more advantages.

Second, you don't need additional lines in the first method. Instead, you now have two methods. Each of them is a little shorter, which makes them easier to understand on their own.

Third, the new method can be reused by other methods. Even if that's not the case right now, you've made the code a little more modular this way.

Fourth, you get a hierarchy of methods: the top-level method getAverageTankFillingPercent() calls the lower-level method roundToIntegerPercent(). This improves the understandability of the higher-level method.

Ideally, each method consists of a series of named statements on a similar level of abstraction. To make this work, we could also extract the code that calculates the average into another utility method. Then we'd have three methods that all work on the same level of indentation.

To sum up, when you replace comments with utility methods, you don't just get rid of a line of text—you can make your code more modular and balance abstraction levels.

Document Implementation Decisions

```java
class Inventory {

    private List<Supply> list = new ArrayList<>();

    void add(Supply supply) {
        list.add(supply);
        Collections.sort(list);
    }

    boolean isInStock(String name) {
        // fast implementation
        return Collections.binarySearch(list, new Supply(name)) != -1;
    }
}
```

Decisions are what make life hard. They do the same to code.

Sometimes you have to make a hard decision in your code—one where there's no objective right or wrong, one that has advantages and disadvantages. This is when you need comments!

Consider the code above. Are you wondering why the programmer decided to use a binarySearch? Well, at least he left us a (helpful) comment: it has to be fast.

The programmer made the decision to use binarySearch, but by saying *yes* to this option, you're saying *no* to a lot of other options. Is the comment really a good justification for this? Think about what *you* would like to know here. And think about what answers the comment gives you.

Here's what we'd like to know: Why is it fast? Why does the code have to be fast? Is the binarySearch method really fast? What costs or trade-offs does this fast solution cause?

And what does the comment state? Well, obviously there are no answers to these questions. So how could we improve this?

Take a look at the new and extended comment:

```
class Inventory {
    // Keep this list sorted. See isInStock().
    private List<Supply> list = new ArrayList<>();

    void add(Supply supply) {
        list.add(supply);
        Collections.sort(list);
    }

    boolean isInStock(String name) {
        /*
         * In the context of checking availability of supplies by name,
         * facing severe performance issues with >1000 supplies
         * we decided to use the binary search algorithm
         * to achieve item retrieval within 1 second,
         * accepting that we must keep the supplies sorted.
         */
        return Collections.binarySearch(list, new Supply(name)) != -1;
    }
}
```

Now that comment is a lot more informative. It states the use case, concerns, the solution, and also any trade-offs or costs we have to pay.

The comment isn't just more helpful now. It's also easy to write. We simply used a template[1] and filled in the necessary bits. Take a look at it:

```
In the context of [USE CASE],
facing [CONCERN]
we decided for [OPTION]
to achieve [QUALITY],
accepting [DOWNSIDE].
```

You can easily spot this structure and find it in this code. With such a template, you're less likely to forget important aspects. What's more, it's going to be easier for your fellow developers to understand comments that follow a clear and predefined structure. This is a point where team conventions pay off.

Our tip: Use this template for documenting important decisions or tricky parts of your code. It needn't be exactly the one you see here, but convention helps. So the first time you bump into this in a project, have a team meeting and decide on your project template! And be sure to mark affected places in your code as well, just as we did with the comment for the list field.

---

1. This template is actually a scientific recommendation from *Sustainable Architectural Design Decisions [ZCTZ13]*. More templates are available on adr.github.io.

Document Using Examples

```
class Supply {

    /**
     * The code universally identifies a supply.
     *
     * It follows a strict format, beginning with an S (for supply), followed
     * by a five digit inventory number. Next comes a backslash that
     * separates the country code from the preceding inventory number. This
     * country code must be exactly two capital letters standing for one of
     * the participating nations (US, EU, RU, CN). After that follows a dot
     * and the actual name of the supply in lowercase letters.
     */
    static final Pattern CODE =
            Pattern.compile("^S\\d{5}\\\\(US|EU|RU|CN)\\.[a-z]+$");
}
```

Some programming constructs are very powerful, but also very complex. Regular expressions fall into this category. You should document complex constructs in a way that makes them easier to understand.

Above, you see a lengthy regular expression. Its name, CODE, doesn't help you to understand what it's good for, but there's also a lengthy comment.

This might seem like a good solution. After all, at least there's a comment and not just the code. The comment describes the sort of strings that the regex will match, and the code even takes care that the regex is compiled exactly once.

The problem isn't that the documentation is wrong (it's not). The problem is that it's less precise than it should be, and it only duplicates what a skilled developer can already read from the regex code itself.

"Lead by example" is always good advice. This comes in very handy for documenting a regex.

Comment Mode

You can also add comments within your regular expressions like this: B[1-9]# Beta Release Numbers. For that to work, you need to pass in the Pattern.COMMENTS flag. Those comments can help, especially for long and complex regular expressions, but we think that examples are even more helpful.

Take a look at how we can improve the documentation:

```
class Supply {

    /**
     * The expression universally identifies a supply code.
     *
     * Format: "S<inventory-number>\<COUNTRY-CODE>.<name>"
     *
     * Valid examples: "S12345\US.pasta", "S08342\CN.wrench",
     * "S88888\EU.laptop", "S12233\RU.brush"
     *
     * Invalid examples:
     * "R12345\RU.fuel"       (Resource, not supply)
     * "S1234\US.light"       (Need five digits)
     * "S01234\AI.coconut"    (Wrong country code. Use US, EU, RU, or CN)
     * " S88888\EU.laptop "   (Trailing whitespaces)
     */
    static final Pattern SUPPLY_CODE =
            Pattern.compile("^S\\d{5}\\\\(US|EU|RU|CN)\\.[a-z]+$");
}
```

The comment above is a little more lengthy, but it's also more structured, and it provides a lot more information. In a nutshell, it describes the format in semi-natural language, and it gives several valid and invalid examples.

The starting sentence is the same as before, but the Format: part condenses the content of the prior example into a single line. This line's just a variation of the code, but with the actual semantics instead of regex syntax. <inventory-number> is just so much more understandable than \d{5}. The parts that are just syntax, such as \ or ., don't need a further explanation.

Next, there are concrete examples. Usually, a valid example lets you understand the expression within a second. That's not something that the code or a lengthy explanation does. The invalid examples are a good quick reference when something goes wrong.

Sure, examples don't usually cover all possible cases. But they're good enough in 90 percent of all cases, and you'll find them so much easier to understand. Plus, we think you should add those examples as unit tests!

Last, we've also taken the opportunity to give the variable a more meaningful name, SUPPLY_CODE.

Structure JavaDoc of Packages

```
/**
 * This package called logistics contains classes for logistics.
 * The inventory class in this package can stock up from the cargo ship and
 * dispose of any contaminated supplies.
 * Classes of this package:
 * - Inventory
 * - Supply
 * - Hull
 * - CargoShip
 * - SupplyCrate
 *
 * @author A. Lien, H. Uman
 * @version 1.8
 * @since 1.7
 */
package logistics;
```

JavaDoc[2] is *the* documentation facility for APIs in Java. You use it to document anything that's public in your code, including packages. If you're writing an API and you want others to use it, that's a must.

Here we have the JavaDoc of the logistics package.[3] At first glance, the JavaDoc comment above looks good, doesn't it? It starts with a nice short summary sentence followed by more details and a list of all the classes in the package. It even uses special annotations to mark the @author, the @version of the current release, and the version @since when this package was added. But at second and third glance, we can spot a lot of issues here!

The summary sentence is basically superfluous. We might write that if we got paid for the number of words, and not for their quality.

The rest of the description is really too abstract. How would we actually use the classes in the package? And is a list of all the classes really needed? No, it's not! JavaDoc generates this automatically anyway.

Last, the annotations aren't really useful either. They duplicate information that's in the version control system anyway. Who will keep this in sync with the code? Hands up, anyone?

In summary, most of the information here is superfluous and unnecessary. Instead, you can get it from the source directly.

---

2. http://www.oracle.com/technetwork/articles/java/index-137868.html
3. You need to put the JavaDoc for packages into a package-info.java file. Similarly, for modules in Java 9, there's the dedicated module-info.java file.

But what should a package JavaDoc documentation contain? Here's what we recommend:

```
/**
 * Classes for managing an inventory of supplies.
 *
 * <p>
 * The core class is the {@link logistics.Inventory} that lets you
 * <ul>
 * <li> stock it up from a {@link logistics.CargoShip},
 * <li> dispose of any contaminated {@link logistics.Supply},
 * <li> and search for any {@link logistics.Supply} by name.
 * </ul>
 *
 * <p>
 * The classes let you unload supplies and immediately dispose of any supply
 * that was contaminated.
 * <pre>
 * Inventory inventory = new Inventory();
 * inventory.stockUp(cargoShip.unload());
 * inventory.disposeContaminatedSupplies();
 * inventory.getContaminatedSupplies().isEmpty(); // true
 * </pre>
 */
package logistics;
```

There are three parts here, separated by vertical space, and no more superfluous information.

The introductory sentence provides a (very) short summary of what you can achieve with the classes in this package.

The second part describes what you can get done with the most important classes in this package. This gives you the starting point for looking deeper into the package and also a pretty good idea whether you need it. And by using the @link annotation, you can simply click on the class and jump directly to it—the JavaDoc tool even checks that linked classes exist when it generates the documentation.

Instead of annotations like @author, which capture information that is in the version control system anyway, we provide a concrete example of how to implement the most important use case in the third part. That's something a developer can use instantaneously.

A good package documentation can really make a difference in understandability. It lowers the entry barrier to all classes in the package. Make sure your API's well documented, and chances are you'll get more stars on Github!

Structure JavaDoc of Classes and Interfaces

```
/**
 * This class represents a cargo ship.
 * It can unload a {@link Stack} of supplies, load a {@link Queue} of
 * supplies, and it can show the remainingCapacity as a long.
 */
interface CargoShip {
    Stack<Supply> unload();
    Queue<Supply> load(Queue<Supply> supplies);
    int getRemainingCapacity();
}
```

Chances are you already know this, but you should document every public class or interface with JavaDoc. This is a rule in practically all Java projects.

The problem is that developers usually write JavaDoc last when their deadline is looming. If that happens, it might look like the comment above. And on the surface, it looks okay.

The JavaDoc comment contains both—a short summary and a more detailed description of the capabilities of the class. It even uses the @link annotation to connect to the data structure classes used.

But similar to the *Structure JavaDoc of Packages*, on page 50, it's lacking structure. The summary and the details are located right next to each other without vertical separation. This makes it harder to identify them as separate. But not only that, there are even errors in the comment.

The summary sentence simply repeats the name of the interface, and that doesn't add much value. Even worse, it's wrong, because CargoShip is an interface and not a class as the comment says.

The detailed description simply restates the method signatures of the interface. This can quickly get out of sync with the actual code: getRemainingCapacity() no longer returns a long value.

So how can we write a helpful comment that doesn't just repeat the interface with its method signatures?

```
/**
 * A cargo ship can load and unload supplies according to its capacity.
 *
 * <p>
 * Supplies are loaded sequentially and can be unloaded in LIFO
 * (last-in-first-out) order. The cargo ship can only store supplies up to
 * its capacity. Its capacity is never negative.
 */
interface CargoShip {
    Stack<Supply> unload();
    Queue<Supply> load(Queue<Supply> supplies);
    int getRemainingCapacity();
}
```

Now the summary sentence is clearly standing out at the top of the JavaDoc comment. And it conveys helpful advice without just reiterating the name of the interface.

The following description provides more details about its behavior: using last-in-first-out, for instance.

What's more, it states two conditions that the interface guarantees to the caller regarding its capacity. You might know such conditions from the JavaDoc comments of the java.util.List interface or other interfaces and classes with state. You call these conditions invariants because they never become false.

So here's our recommendation for good JavaDoc comments for interfaces and public classes: First, start with a short and concise summary. Separate this vertically from invariants the class or interface guarantees. Don't just duplicate method signatures.

And examples always help! So sit down and have a go at an example for how to use the interface above.

Structure JavaDoc of Methods

```java
interface CargoShip {

    Stack<Supply> unload();

    /**
     * Loads {@link Supply}.
     *
     * @param supplies the supplies of type {@link Queue}
     * @return not loaded supplies of type {@link Queue}
     */
    Queue<Supply> load(Queue<Supply> supplies);

    int getRemainingCapacity();
}
```

From classes and interfaces (*Structure JavaDoc of Classes and Interfaces*, on page 52), we are now moving one level deeper to JavaDoc comments for methods.

Methods represent the behavior of objects. By calling methods, you trigger state changes and side effects. That's why documenting methods with JavaDoc is more important than any other kind of JavaDoc comments. You can even see that in most modern IDEs. They guide the programmer when selecting a method to call with a quick extract from the method's JavaDoc comment. They'll usually also support a quick lookup function for JavaDoc.

Do you notice the summary sentence and the @link annotations used here? As so many times before, they don't add much helpful information in the comment.

And what about the other two lines in the comment—the input parameter marked with @param and the return value marked with @return? Here the comment describes nothing new—it just repeats the method signature.

So is this comment enough? Do you know what happens when you pass null instead of a Queue instance? Can a runtime exception occur for certain inputs?

No. No. And no idea. We have no clue how the method will behave, even though there's a JavaDoc comment. So if we use this method, we're no longer certain how our code will behave. That would be especially problematic if you're building an API.

Let's see what we can do about it:

```java
interface CargoShip {

    Stack<Supply> unload();

    /**
     * Loads supplies onto the cargo ship.
     *
     * <p>
     * Only lets you load as many supplies as there is remaining capacity.
     *
     * Example:
     * <pre>
     * int capacity = cargoShip.getRemainingCapacity(); // 1
     * Queue&lt;Supply> supplies = Arrays.asList(new Supply("Apple"));
     * Queue&lt;Supply> spareSupplies = cargoShip.load(supplies);
     * spareSupplies.isEmpty(); // true;
     * cargoShip.getRemainingCapacity() == 0; // true
     * </pre>
     *
     * @param supplies to be loaded; must not be null
     * @return supplies that could not be loaded because of too little
     *          capacity; is empty if everything has been loaded
     * @throws NullPointerException if supplies is null
     * @see CargoShip#getRemainingCapacity() check capacity
     * @see CargoShip#unload() unload the supplies
     */
    Queue<Supply> load(Queue<Supply> supplies);

    int getRemainingCapacity();
}
```

This is much better now. The JavaDoc comment reads like a contract. It states how the input and its internal state must be to guarantee a certain output and state change.

The contract covers a good case with a description and a code example. Note that the < characters must be escaped with < because <pre> is an XML environment.

Even invalid input, such as null, is specified in the @param description, along with the consequences of a violation: @throws a NullPointerException.

What's more, the comment refers to other methods via the @see annotation. It describes how you can undo the effects of the method or observe state changes caused by calling the method.

Just keep this in mind: the contract metaphor doesn't fully apply—you can't usually sue someone if the implementation differs from its specification.

Structure JavaDoc of Constructors

```java
class Inventory {

    List<Supply> supplies;

    /**
     * Constructor for a new Inventory.
     */
    Inventory() {
        this(new ArrayList<>());
    }

    /**
     * Another Constructor for a new Inventory.
     *
     * It is possible to add some supplies to the Inventory.
     */
    Inventory(Collection<Supply> initialSupplies) {
        this.supplies = new ArrayList<>(initialSupplies);
    }
}
```

There's one special type of method in Java that you can't assign a good and meaningful name to: constructors. They always have the same name as the class. They may have a clearer purpose than other methods (they always construct an object), but if you misuse them, those objects will be flawed. That's why you have to explain constructors with good and informative JavaDoc comments.

In the example above, the JavaDoc is poorly done. Neither of the summary sentences really carry new information, and they are rather obsolete. The second sentence in the lower constructor also misses the point. How are the supplies added exactly? Does the addition refer to the parameter initialSupplies or is there another method for that?

Also, there's no hint on how the two constructors are related to each other. Normally when you use a third-party class, you don't read the sources—only the JavaDoc. That's why the JavaDoc comment of a constructor[4] must explain everything necessary for a programmer to use it.

---

4. Sometimes, however, it's easier to hide the constructor alltogether and expose a meaningfully named static method that invokes the hidden constructor internally—a so-called factory method.

So what do you have to know to use this class correctly?

```java
class Inventory {

    List<Supply> supplies;

    /**
     * Creates an empty inventory.
     *
     * @see Inventory#Inventory(Collection) instantiate with initial supplies
     */
    Inventory() {
        this(new ArrayList<>());
    }

    /**
     * Creates an inventory with an initial shipment of supplies.
     *
     * @param initialSupplies Initial supplies.
     *                        Must not be null, can be empty.
     * @throws NullPointerException if initialSupplies is null
     * @see Inventory#Inventory() instantiate with no supplies
     */
    Inventory(Collection<Supply> initialSupplies) {
        this.supplies = new ArrayList<>(initialSupplies);
    }
}
```

The first and most important thing you need to know is how to call a constructor correctly. You especially need to know what preconditions you have to fulfill so that everything works out as desired. The default constructor doesn't really have preconditions and no input parameter, but the second one does: a Collection of Supply objects called initialSupplies. We have to document this one like we do with other method parameters. Here, you're not allowed to enter null, and if you do, then you get a NullPointerException back. The comment states this in the @throws part.

Second, you need information about the state of the object when the constructor finishes, because its state determines which other methods you can call at this point. That's called a postcondition. In the code above, the inventory's either going to be in an "empty" state or filled with "initial supplies." The summary sentences of both constructors describe that.

But there's even more in the comments: two @see annotations. These annotations provide hints to the developer. They outline alternatives that she may not have seen otherwise. Here, we use these annotations to explain the relationship between the two constructors.

Because constructors lack a name, their JavaDoc is just so important!

What Have You Learned?

In this chapter, you learned when and how to write helpful comments. This might seem so unimportant. After all, who cares about something that the compiler deletes?

In fact, it's quite the opposite! Good comments can help you make your code base more readable and easier to understand. They can be a superb way of helping the future maintainer—that is, as long as you apply them only when they're really needed and in a way that actually helps.

That's why we started this chapter by going over when you should use comments and when you should get rid of them. You've learned that it's always good to remove superfluous comments and even commented-out code. After all, the version control system won't forget it. Now you can also transform comments into code by extracting constants or utility methods. This gives you more support from the compiler.

But it is not just about removing comments, of course! You also learned to structure your documentation in a way that helps others, whether you are explaining the design decisions for your implementation or a regular expression.

Since documentation is also about conventions, we showed you how you can leverage JavaDoc to build well-documented packages, interfaces, and methods.

We're still far from done! As you've seen here, conventions help you to write understandable documentation. But you can still confuse everybody if your variables are all named x, y, and z. Surely you remember your math lessons in school? In the next chapter, we'll show you how to assign good names to code structures so that other Java developers have an easy time understanding.

There are only two hard problems in Computer Science: cache invalidation and naming things.

▸ *Phil Karlton*

CHAPTER 4

Name Things Right

In Norwegian, the term for "moose" is "elg." When the first northern settlers from Europe came to North America and saw this huge elg-like animal in the forest, they decided: "Okay, that's gonna be the elg here" (or elk, as it's spelled in English). Turns out, they were completely wrong. The settlers happened to meet a wapiti first—a totally different kind of deer. There is a close relative to the European "elg" in North America, but it's the moose. Up to the present day, this little naming error leads to profound confusion between North American and European friends of the wilderness, and it leads to a discussion on etymology at the start of every "elg tour" in Scandinavia.

Assigning good names can be very hard. Even experts have a difficult time coming up with a good name on the first try. The European settlers had a concept for moose, but they still managed to assign it to the wrong animal.

Naming's even harder for your code. Code doesn't have horns or other properties that most people would recognize. It's abstract, and most of the time, it's also completely new and very domain-specific.

That's why good naming is more important in programming. We have to name a whole lot of stuff: packages, classes, methods, fields, parameters, and local variables. And these elements often represent something unknown or hard to grasp. This makes it very difficult to find a good name, especially in the beginning. Later, after using an element a lot, you may find it easier to come up with a better name because you'll be able to relate to the concept easily.

The comparisons in this section help you find better names for your code elements. We'll show you why the Java conventions matter when it comes to naming, why you should be concise when naming methods, and how to avoid meaningless or single letter names.

Use Java Naming Conventions

```
class Rover {
    static final double WalkingSpeed = 3;

    final String SerialNumber;
    double MilesPerHour;

    Rover(String NewSerialNumber) {
        SerialNumber = NewSerialNumber;
    }

    void Drive() {
        MilesPerHour = WalkingSpeed;
    }
    void Stop() {
        MilesPerHour = 0;
    }
}
```

We have to name a lot of *stuff* in Java: packages, classes, interfaces, enums, methods, variables, fields, parameters, and constants. Take a look at the code above—it contains a lot of names. Do you notice anything strange? Can you see the pattern?

We consistently named everything in CamelCase: no spaces, and all words start with a capital letter. As long as we're consistent, we can choose any way of naming, can't we?

Well, in theory yes, but not in practice! The Java code out there that counts as professional follows a different style. To us, the code above isn't just hard to read—it even feels horribly wrong. Just to be clear: There's no functional error. But to a Java programmer, this doesn't read like Java code.

But What About Package Names?

Yes, you caught us. We didn't cover package names in the code snippets. We never do in this book, actually. But they're important, too. Packages act like global namespaces, and you shouldn't have name clashes where a package has the same identifier as another package. On the Internet, the Domain Name System (DNS) is *the* largest global namespace we know. Because we programmers don't want to reinvent the wheel over and over again, we usually simply convert domain names into package names. For example, the URL of our book pragprog.com/book/javacomp results in the package name com.pragprog.book.javacomp. Just like in domain names, we don't use capital letters in Java package names either.

How can we change the code so that it also looks like Java?

```java
class Rover {
    static final double WALKING_SPEED = 3;

    final String serialNumber;
    double milesPerHour;

    Rover(String serialNumber) {
        this.serialNumber = serialNumber;
    }

    void drive() {
        milesPerHour = WALKING_SPEED;
    }

    void stop() {
        milesPerHour = 0;
    }
}
```

Since 1997, we have the Java code conventions.[1] These conventions are the *de facto* standard for formatting Java code, including names.

Above, we changed the code to conform to the Java code conventions. We kept the name of the class because it already follows the conventions: it's written in CamelCase, beginning with a capital letter and starting every term in the name with a capital letter. Interfaces and enums work likewise.

To let the constants (variables that are final and static) stand out, you should write their names in CAPITAL_SNAKE_CASE. This means that all letters in the name are uppercase, and you separate terms with an underscore. That way, the name of the constant already scream out *"I won't change."*

Methods, fields, parameters, and variables use a variant of camelCase where the first letter starts in lowercase. This has the downside of a possible confusion of method (behavior) and variable (state) names since they're named in the same scheme. That's why their name itself should tell the reader if it's a method or a variable. You should name your methods as verbs, as you see in drive() in the code above, or let them start with verbs like is, has, save, get, or set, *etc.* For variables, use nouns, such as serialNumber or milesPerHour.

The Java code conventions are only the very first step in good naming. The point is that you'll never have a good name if it doesn't follow the conventions (the reverse, a bad name that follows the conventions, is entirely possible and all too common). Conventions are a basic requirement.

---

1. http://www.oracle.com/technetwork/java/codeconventions-150003.pdf

Follow Getter/Setter Conventions for Frameworks

```
class Astronaut {
    String name;
    boolean retired;

    Astronaut(String name) {
        this.name = name;
    }

    String getFullName() {
        return name;
    }
    void setFullName(String name) {
        this.name = name;
    }

    boolean getRetired() {
        return retired;
    }

    void setRetiredState(boolean retired) {
        this.retired = retired;
    }
}
```

In object-oriented programming languages, you usually try to avoid direct access to the fields of a class from the outside. That's why you write getter and setter methods that control this access.

The structure and naming of getters and setters is so standardized that many frameworks heavily rely on it. Hibernate uses it to convert Java instances and rows in a SQL database, Jackson uses it for JSON messages, and even the Play Framework uses it for building HTML forms. That's why getters and setters have a specification of their own, the JavaBeans specification.[2] We call classes that follow that convention JavaBeans and yes, it somehow stretches that coffee metaphor of Java.

Take a look at the code above. Does every field have a correctly named getter and setter? Is there a constructor without any parameters? Are the visibility levels correct?

No, they're not. Strange things can happen when you use instances of that class within frameworks. Most frameworks won't throw exceptions but will fail silently—or simply work in ways you didn't expect.

---

2. http://download.oracle.com/otndocs/jcp/7224-javabeans-1.01-fr-spec-oth-JSpec/

So what do we need to change to turn this class into a JavaBean?

```java
class Astronaut {
    private String name;
    private boolean retired;

    public Astronaut() {
    }

    public Astronaut(String name) {
        this.name = name;
    }

    public String getName() {
        return name;
    }

    public void setName(String name) {
        this.name = name;
    }

    public boolean isRetired() {
        return retired;
    }

    public void setRetired(boolean retired) {
        this.retired = retired;
    }

}
```

We've reworked the code in a number of ways. Now the class above is a valid JavaBean. First, we changed the modifiers of the fields to private and the getters and setters to public.[3] This ensures that frameworks will use the getters and setters and won't circumvent them by accessing fields directly.

Next, we added a default constructor. Most frameworks need this to create a blank instance of a class, which they configure by calling setters to assign values to fields. You can easily overlook this part because the default constructor isn't available anymore if you add another one with parameters.

And last, we renamed the setters and getters to reflect the name of the field. If the field has the name foo then the getter and setter should be named getFoo() and setFoo(). Be aware that this changes slightly for a boolean field. The name of the setter stays the same, but the getter turns to isFoo() instead—it reads like a question. Too bad Java doesn't allow us to put a question mark there.

One last note: We're not saying that JavaBeans are a great way of writing code, but you'll have to use them for some frameworks in Java.

---

3. We're avoiding modifiers in other parts of the book, but here they really matter.

Avoid Single-Letter Names

```
class Inventory {
    List<Supply> sl = new ArrayList<>();

    boolean isInStock(String n) {
        Supply s = new Supply(n);
        int l = 0;
        int h = sl.size() - 1;

        while (l <= h) {
            int m = l + (h - l) / 2;
            int c = sl.get(m).compareTo(s);

            if (c < 0) {
                l = m + 1;
            } else if (c > 0) {
                h = m - 1;
            } else {
                return true;
            }
        }

        return false;
    }
}
```

In most code bases, you'll often find a variable whose name is just a single letter. They're common because they're quicker to type and because some IDEs still generate names in this way. But they make the code much harder to read. After all, how much meaning can you convey in a single letter?

Let's look at the code above. It shows an Inventory class with the method isInStock. All variables inside this method have single letter names: n, l, h, m, c, s.

Can you understand what's going on inside the method? Actually, it's just an ordinary binary search. But we're having a hard time reading that from the code because of the variable names.

There's no excuse for using single-letter names. Although some theorists would like it to be so, code is much more than pure math. An average programmer reads thousands of lines of code per day. This task doesn't get easier if everywhere she looks, variables have the same names, which aren't connected to the context of a piece of code. That's why we should put meaning in variable names, and we can't do that with just one letter.

On a side note: The code uses the lowercase letter l and the number 1. They're very hard to distinguish in most fonts. Our advice: Simply avoid the single letter l as a variable name. Same for the uppercase O and the number 0.

So let's see what difference longer variable names can make.

```java
class Inventory {
    List<Supply> sortedList = new ArrayList<>();

    boolean isInStock(String name) {
        Supply supply = new Supply(name);
        int low = 0;
        int high = sortedList.size() - 1;

        while (low <= high) {
            int middle = low + (high - low) / 2;
            int comparison = sortedList.get(middle).compareTo(supply);

            if (comparison < 0) {
                low = middle + 1;
            } else if (comparison > 0) {
                high = middle - 1;
            } else {
                return true;
            }
        }

        return false;
    }
}
```

Astonishing, isn't it? Without full names, every reader would have to build and remember the following table in her mind:

n	name	m	middle	sl	sortedList
l	low	c	comparison		
h	high	s	supply		

We can just cut out the table by using full names directly in code. And there's no downside to this solution. Some people are afraid that longer names make the code less efficient, but this just isn't true. The compiler replaces the names anyway on compilation, and in bytecode, full names and single-letter names look the same. The difference is that bytecode's only read by machines, not by humans.

As we mentioned above, the code uses binary search. This makes it a perfect candidate for more improvements, for example, to *Document Implementation Decisions*, on page 46 or *Favor Java API Over DIY*, on page 34. We could also *Replace Magic Numbers with Constants*, on page 20.

Avoid Abbreviations

```
class Logbook {
    static final Path DIR = Paths.get("/var/log");
    static final Path CSV = DIR.resolve("stats.csv");
    static final String GLOB = "*.log";

    void createStats() throws IOException {
        try (DirectoryStream<Path> dirStr =
                    Files.newDirectoryStream(DIR, GLOB);
            BufferedWriter bufW = Files.newBufferedWriter(CSV)) {
            for (Path lFile : dirStr) {
                String csvLn = String.format("%s,%d,%s",
                        lFile,
                        Files.size(lFile),
                        Files.getLastModifiedTime(lFile));
                bufW.write(csvLn);
                bufW.newLine();
            }
        }
    }
}
```

Abbreviations are one step up from single-letter names, and our world is full of them: ASAP, FYI, TGIF, AFK, NASA, FBI, CYA, NYPD, and so on. Many programmers like to create their own abbreviations in their code. The obvious problem is that they're the only ones who know those abbreviations—everyone else has to learn them first. And learning takes time. That's why it's better to avoid abbreviations altogether so that others can grasp the code more quickly (and have fewer WTF moments[4]).

You can read a lot of abbreviations in the code above: DIR, CSV, GLOB, dirStr, bufW, lFile, and csvLn. Do you know immediately what they refer to? For some you might, but probably not for all.

Out of context, it's hard to determine what bufW or dirStr means. Together with the variable types BufferedWriter and DirectoryStream it becomes more obvious, but it's still unnecessarily hard.

And what the heck does GLOB stand for? It's actually a way to refer to sets of file paths common in Unix environments, which is what the code above is for—for example, all Java files via *.java. But you have to know that first.

Sometimes people abbreviate only parts of a variable: lFile or csvLn. We have to channel our inner Sherlock Holmes to figure out what the l or Ln mean.

---

4. http://www.osnews.com/story/19266/WTFs_m

So what should we do with abbreviations?

```
class Logbook {
    static final Path LOG_FOLDER = Paths.get("/var/log");
    static final Path STATISTICS_CSV = LOG_FOLDER.resolve("stats.csv");
    static final String FILE_FILTER = "*.log";

    void createStatistics() throws IOException {
        try (DirectoryStream<Path> logs =
                    Files.newDirectoryStream(LOG_FOLDER, FILE_FILTER);
             BufferedWriter writer =
                    Files.newBufferedWriter(STATISTICS_CSV)) {
            for (Path log : logs) {
                String csvLine = String.format("%s,%d,%s",
                        log,
                        Files.size(log),
                        Files.getLastModifiedTime(log));
                writer.write(csvLine);
                writer.newLine();
            }
        }
    }
}
```

The rule is quite obvious: only use abbreviations that are very common, and use long names for the rest.

Just look at the code above. It's much easier to comprehend, and we don't stumble upon strange variable names anymore.

First, we renamed the three fields from DIR, CSV, and GLOB to LOG_FOLDER, STATISTICS_CSV, and FILE_FILTER. In our view, CSV (comma-separated values) is the only abbreviation in the code that's sufficiently well-known. We kept it and added a little bit more context to it. Next, we replaced the abbreviations DIR and GLOB with concise unabbreviated names. FILE_FILTER conveys the variable's intent much better than GLOB.

You don't always have to spell out abbreviations in full. For bufW, the full name would be bufferedWriter. We just use the second word writer because that's its purpose here. The fact that it has a buffer is less important. And as the replacement for dirStr, the short name logs seems much more informative than the full name directoryStream.

Lastly, we renamed the variable csvLn to csvLine. Its purpose is to indicate that it contains a line (of a CSV file), so why shouldn't we just call it line, too?

To sum up, you should try to avoid abbreviations and use them only if they're *very* common. If in doubt, *spell it out!*

Avoid Meaningless Terms

```
class MainSpaceShipManager {
    AbstractRocketPropulsionEngine abstractRocketPropulsionEngine;
    INavigationController navigationController;
    boolean turboEnabledFlag;

    void navigateSpaceShipTo(PlanetInfo planetInfo) {
        RouteData data = navigationController.calculateRouteData(planetInfo);
        LogHelper.logRouteData(data);
        abstractRocketPropulsionEngine.invokeTask(data, turboEnabledFlag);
    }
}
```

Good naming isn't just about spelling out short names and making names longer. Sometimes, long names can be just as burdensome. And there are some terms programmers use often that have lost all meaning.

Look at the code above. It doesn't contain abbreviations like in *Avoid Abbreviations*, on page 66, and all names are spelled out, but that doesn't mean the naming is good. There are various meaningless words in there that you can just remove. And we've seen names like this many times in real production code.

Can you spot which words convey no meaning and just add text? What parts could you leave out without impacting understandability?

There are some low-hanging fruits—meaningless terms that people use very often, like "main," "manager," "data," "info," or "flag." They're easy to spot. But what about the terms "abstract," a method named "invoke," or a parameter's type within a method name? Are those meaningful? Not really.

Brevity and Naming: The Eternal Struggle

Brevity in naming isn't necessarily a virtue. Most often, it's better to have a verbose but descriptive name instead of a cryptic abbreviation whose only benefit is that it's easy to type. Normally, you won't type a full name anyway. Your IDE's auto-completion will do this for you. And we have to emphasize: names are read much more often than they're written. If a name is confusing, misleading, wrong, hard to understand, or missing the right information, a new developer will have a hard time working with the code.

So what parts can we leave out without losing the intended meaning?

```
class SpaceShip {
    Engine engine;
    Navigator navigator;
    boolean turboEnabled;

    void navigateTo(Planet destination) {
        Route route = navigator.calculateRouteTo(destination);
        Logger.log(route);
        engine.follow(route, turboEnabled);
    }
}
```

Actually, we can leave out a lot. Just compare the two code snippets: we removed over 100 characters (about a quarter of the whole code). That's a lot less to read and think about. Not bad! Let's go through it.

To start with, we simply removed typical meaningless terms like "data," "info," or "flag." It's rare that such terms add any meaning to the code.

Next, when reading a type name, we don't care if it's an enum, a class, an interface, or an abstract class. After all, the type itself is already stating this. That's why the term "abstract" or "impl" doesn't help in class names, and neither the prefix "I" for names of interfaces. Don't do this!

A class's name provides context to its members and already conveys a lot of meaning. That's why you can remove domain specifiers like "rocket" in a class named "SpaceShip." You can do the same with repeated parameter types in method names, as in logRouteData(), which we renamed to log(). The parameter route itself already states what's being logged—no need to repeat it in the method name.

Verbs like "invoke," "call," or "do" also convey little meaning in method names. Instead of using these, you should try to find a more precise and meaningful verb instead. Lastly, we often see meaningless terms in package names as well. Watch out for words like misc, other, or util.

Our advice is to watch out for the terms mentioned here and to think twice whenever you feel tempted to write them. Whether a term is actually meaningful or not depends on the concrete context. Many frameworks have a hard time deciding this as well. One class name in the Spring framework is famous: *Roses are red, leaves are green, but only Java has AbstractSingletonProxyFactoryBean.*[5]

---

5. http://www.bash.org/?962108

Use Domain Terminology

```java
class Person {
    String lastName;
    String role;
    int travels;
    LocalDate employedSince;

    String serializeAsLine() {
        return String.join(",",
                Arrays.asList(lastName,
                        role,
                        String.valueOf(travels),
                        String.valueOf(employedSince))
        );
    }
}
```

The code you work on usually belongs to a specific domain, and a domain has its own vocabulary. Think of sports; different sports have their own domain-specific names for hurling, throwing, kicking, bending, or dunking a different kind of ball. The more you insert the terms of your program's domain into your code, the better.

In the code above, you see a class for representing a person with a last name, a role, the number of travels, and the date of employment. The class is quite generic, and you can probably find something similar in most systems that store employee data. You might still wonder why the code uses exactly these attributes. Why does it only consider the last name and not also the first name? And why does it track the number of travels?

The name of the method, serializeAsLine(), is quite generic, too. From that name, we only know that this person's fields are serialized to a string without line breaks. But we don't know if there's something specific about the format.

Are All Names Equally Important?

Good names matter, but the short answer is still no. As a rule of thumb, the larger the scope of name, the higher its importance. The reason for that is simple: a name with a large scope, such as a class or a package, is much more likely to be read in comparison to a name with a small scope, such as a variable within a method. That's why you should put more effort into more important names.

Take a look at how domain-specific naming improves the readability of the code:

```
class Astronaut {
    String tagName;
    String rank;
    int missions;
    LocalDate activeDutySince;

    String toCSV() {
        return String.join(",",
                Arrays.asList(tagName,
                    rank,
                    String.valueOf(missions),
                    String.valueOf(activeDutySince))
        );
    }
}
```

In this book, we put the code examples in a domain inspired by a Mars mission, and we fit all the names into this particular domain. This automatically makes the code much clearer.

When it's put into context, the meaning of the different attributes is much easier to understand. First of all, we want to store data about an Astronaut and not just a Person, and that should be obvious from the class name. Of course, an astronaut is also a person in real life, but we're only interested in astronaut-related aspects. In this setting, the lastname is meant to be the writing on the tag an astronaut is wearing, the role actually refers to the rank she's in, and now travels is also much clearer since it's supposed to refer to the number of missions in space. In the same fashion, employedSince actually refers to the activeDutySince.

But the Mars mission isn't the only domain in the class. Code deals with technical concepts, which means that you're always implicitly in a technical domain with its own terminology. Because of this, we renamed the method serializeAsLine() as toCSV(). After all, the resulting format of the serialized representation of an astronaut is a line of comma-separated values. This makes the meaning of the method more obvious to most programmers, simply because the term CSV is very common in the programming domain, as we've seen in *Avoid Abbreviations*, on page 66.

To sum up: You should align names in your code to the domain it belongs to as far as possible and avoid generic names.

What Have You Learned?

Naming is one of the hardest tasks that you face in your day-to-day developer life. Bad naming usually doesn't stop your code from compiling (so no compiler will help you to find really bad names), but it'll make the code much harder to read and understand. And that can turn the maintenance of your code into a nightmare.

That's why we've added this chapter on naming to the book. Good naming is less clear-cut and well defined than the problems you've seen in some of the other comparisons here. In our experience, you're never done with proper naming. When you look at a piece of code that you've written some time ago, chances are you'll find something to improve in naming, if only because you've had more time to get acquainted with the terms of the domain. Our advice is to always refactor when a better name comes to your mind.

When it comes to naming, conventions are half the rent. Even if you come up with a good name, it's going to look bad if it violates the Java conventions. Conventions are especially important for naming getters and setters, which are about the only part of Java where terrible naming can result in compile or runtime errors when you use certain frameworks. But conventions aside, good names shouldn't be too short (be careful with single letters and abbreviations) or too long (packed with meaningless terms), and hitting the right level is really hard. Your best bet is to always align names to the domain you're writing the code for.

In the next chapter, we'll move back to a topic that doesn't just influence the understandability of your code, but also its functional correctness: exception handling. No matter what type of program you write, unforeseen things can happen, and it's your job to prepare for that. But as exception handling breaks the regular control flow, it comes with big potential for introducing subtle bugs or implementing it in a way that's hard to understand. We're going to show you some tips and tricks to avoid that.

CHAPTER 5

Prepare for Things Going Wrong

Do you own a car? Do you have insurance for it? If not, you'd better get a policy now. It can cost you a lot of money, and chances are, you'll drive your car for thousands of miles without any trouble. But it just takes a moment of bad luck to leave you with life-changing consequences. That's why you need insurance to act as a safety net for your really expensive things (cars, houses) and your really important things (your health!).

It's similar with code. Most of the time, your program will execute just fine and take the happy path (the default control-flow path without any exceptional or erroneous conditions). But things can and will go wrong. When they do, you'll need a safety net. If you don't have one, your program could suffer the consequences—it can crash or produce faulty data. Or worst of all, it can continue to run as if nothing happened—you won't see the damage until much later, and by then, you'll have a hard time figuring out what's wrong (not to mention all the data that might have been corrupted by then).

You have to ensure your program against errors even if it's completely bug-free (and it never is). That's because there are things that you just can't control. For example, a user might try to read a file from a broken filesystem. Or the machine where your program is running might be disconnected from the network. Or it might receive malicious messages from a remote host.

In Java, we ensure our program handle errors by catching and throwing exceptions. The comparisons we'll explore in this chapter will show you several important do's and don'ts related to handling exceptions. You will learn how to *fail fast* while collecting as much information about the error as possible (without breaking the exception cause chain) and be explicit about swallowing errors. When handling exceptions, your program will leave the normal path of executions. That's why you need to be sure you *always* close your scarce resources. Remember: It's better to be safe than sorry! Let's begin.

Fail Fast

```
class CruiseControl {
    static final double SPEED_OF_LIGHT_KMH = 1079252850;
    static final double SPEED_LIMIT = SPEED_OF_LIGHT_KMH;

    private double targetSpeedKmh;

    void setTargetSpeedKmh(double speedKmh) {
        if (speedKmh < 0) {
            throw new IllegalArgumentException();
        } else if (speedKmh <= SPEED_LIMIT) {
            targetSpeedKmh = speedKmh;
        } else {
            throw new IllegalArgumentException();
        }
    }
}
```

Let's take a look at the method setTargetSpeedKmh(). The if conditional with its three branches surely does some exception handling. But do you immediately understand why it's structured that way? Probably not.

The normal path in this method is a little bit concealed. It's the second of the three branches surrounded by (or hidden in between) two branches of error handling. We're primarily interested in this normal path, because there lies the actual functionality, and this one will be executed most of the time. The code above wastes precious developer time just for spotting that path between the parameter validation.

When you read those branches sequentially, the last one is troublesome. The first branch is a validation, and the second the normal path. At that point, you might think you know how the method works and what parameters it accepts. But then the last branch comes along with another validation condition. You have to do a mental rollback and update your understanding of the parameter validation. This is a waste of mental energy that's just not necessary.

There's another unnecessary complication in the code. All branches of the conditional are connected so you have to understand all conditions together. This is easy for the first branch with the condition speedKmh <= 0, but it becomes more complicated for the other two. Which condition applies exactly for the second and third branches? It's !(speedKmh <= 0) && speedKmh <= SPEED_LIMIT and !(!(speedKmh <= 0) && speedKmh <= SPEED_LIMIT). No problem for the JVM, but it's not that easy for us humans.

So, how can we make this code more understandable? By failing fast:

```
class CruiseControl {
    static final double SPEED_OF_LIGHT_KMH = 1079252850;
    static final double SPEED_LIMIT = SPEED_OF_LIGHT_KMH;

    private double targetSpeedKmh;

    void setTargetSpeedKmh(double speedKmh) {
        if (speedKmh < 0 || speedKmh > SPEED_LIMIT) {
            throw new IllegalArgumentException();
        }

        targetSpeedKmh = speedKmh;
    }
}
```

We separated the normal path from parameter validations and placed the two combined conditions at the top of the method. If one of them holds, the method returns immediately and throws an IllegalArgumentException. In other words, the method *fails fast*.

Failing fast makes the whole method more readable and understandable! But not only that, we even got rid of one level of indentation for the normal path.

Think of the validation block as the bouncer of your club and the normal path block as the dance area. The bouncer ensures that no underaged party people can enter your club. We trust the bouncer that she's doing her job, so we know we don't need to check again on the dance floor. That means we can concentrate on the normal path without having to recall all validation conditions.

And with that solution, you can immediately spot the two-part structure separated by an empty line. First comes the parameter validation, then the normal path of the method. This means that you can jump right into the most important part of the method—the normal path—and you don't need to read the whole validation logic upfront.

The structure of the method is quite good now, but we can improve this solution even more: we should apply *Explain Cause in Message*, on page 78 and *Simplify Boolean Expressions*, on page 8. Go ahead and try it for yourself!

Always Catch Most Specific Exception

```java
class TransmissionParser {
    static Transmission parse(String rawMessage) {
        if (rawMessage != null
                && rawMessage.length() != Transmission.MESSAGE_LENGTH) {
            throw new IllegalArgumentException("Bad message received!");
        }

        String rawId = rawMessage.substring(0, Transmission.ID_LENGTH);
        String rawContent = rawMessage.substring(Transmission.ID_LENGTH);
        try {
            int id = Integer.parseInt(rawId);
            String content = rawContent.trim();
            return new Transmission(id, content);
        } catch (Exception e) {
            throw new IllegalArgumentException("Bad message received!");
        }
    }
}
```

Exceptions in Java are part of a relatively complex type hierarchy. When you catch an exception, you should always catch the most specific exception type. If you catch a more general type, you risk swallowing errors that you shouldn't.

The code above parses a message of type String and dissects it into an id and a content part. The problem lies in the catch statement. Any type of Exception is caught here.

Exception is the most general exception type in Java. The only thing that's even more general is the super type of Exception: Throwable (this comes from the catch and throw metaphor). If you catch a Throwable, you'll even catch errors in the virtual machine, such as OutOfMemoryError. Don't do this!

Many beginners find it tempting to catch a very general type. After all, you consume practically any type of error with a single statement.

But this is only good on the surface. It means that you catch exception types that you don't want to handle here, such as a NullPointerException. In most cases, this exception indicates a bug in your code that you need to fix. When it occurs, you *want* the program to crash so that you become aware of the problem.

Just because you hide a bug by catching an exception doesn't mean it's fixed. It will just bring down your program at a more inconvenient point in time.

So what type of exception should you catch here?

```java
class TransmissionParser {
    static Transmission parse(String rawMessage) {
        if (rawMessage != null &&
                rawMessage.length() != Transmission.MESSAGE_LENGTH) {
            throw new IllegalArgumentException("Bad message received!");
        }

        String rawId = rawMessage.substring(0, Transmission.ID_LENGTH);
        String rawContent = rawMessage.substring(Transmission.ID_LENGTH);
        try {
            int id = Integer.parseInt(rawId);
            String content = rawContent.trim();
            return new Transmission(id, content);
        } catch (NumberFormatException e) {
            throw new IllegalArgumentException("Bad message received!");
        }
    }
}
```

The fix to this problem is very simple. You just need to catch the most specific exception that might be thrown by the code in the try instead of Exception.[1]

There's one specific type of exception that we need to take care of here: NumberFormatException. This one will be thrown by Integer.parseInt(rawId) if rawId contains something that the Integer class can't turn into an integer value. Basically, any nondigit character will cause it.

So all you need to do is replace Exception with NumberFormatException. Then, the code will no longer swallow errors that it shouldn't, such as a NullPointerException.

Sometimes, catching the most specific exception means that you need to catch many exceptions. This might mean that you have to write many catch blocks instead of just a single one. Don't let the fact that more code is needed fool you into believing that catching a general exception type is better! After all, more code with less bugs is better than less code with more bugs.

If you do the same handling for all exceptions, there's also a convenient way to get around multiple catch blocks. Since Java 7, there's the multi-catch block. Say you want to handle a NumberFormatException and an IOException in the same way. Just write catch(NumberFormatException | IOException e) and combine two catch blocks into one. Whichever method you use to structure your catch blocks, be sure to catch the most specific exceptions only.

---

1. Of course, there can be cases where the most specific exception is actually Exception and then catching it is fine. But those cases are very rare.

Explain Cause in Message

```
class TransmissionParser {
    static Transmission parse(String rawMessage) {
        if (rawMessage != null
                && rawMessage.length() != Transmission.MESSAGE_LENGTH) {
            throw new IllegalArgumentException();
        }

        String rawId = rawMessage.substring(0, Transmission.ID_LENGTH);
        String rawContent = rawMessage.substring(Transmission.ID_LENGTH);
        try {
            int id = Integer.parseInt(rawId);
            String content = rawContent.trim();
            return new Transmission(id, content);
        } catch (NumberFormatException e) {
            throw new IllegalArgumentException("Bad message received!");
        }
    }
}
```

Exception handling is not only about catching exceptions, but also about throwing them. When throwing an exception, you should follow type conventions to make handling of the exception easier.

The type of an exception already describes *what* is wrong: bad parameters of a method cause an IllegalArgumentException; reading a nonexistent file causes a FileNotFoundException. But the type alone isn't enough because it lacks the context: which parameter is wrong and why? Which file isn't available on the filesystem?

We can only fix bugs that we can reproduce. Otherwise, we don't know whether we really fixed them. Typically, we start with the stack trace of an exception and trace our way back in the code until we find the root cause. If the exception itself provides a detailed context, this is much easier.

The exceptions thrown in the code above, however, lack context. The first IllegalArgumentException is created with the default constructor and provides no context at all. The second one comes with a message as input for the constructor, but it's not really helpful. Sadly, messages of this type are very common.

We suggest giving them a bit more thought.

So how can we include the context within the message of the exceptions?

```
class TransmissionParser {
    static Transmission parse(String rawMessage) {
        if (rawMessage != null
                && rawMessage.length() != Transmission.MESSAGE_LENGTH) {
            throw new IllegalArgumentException(
                String.format("Expected %d, but got %d characters in '%s'",
                    Transmission.MESSAGE_LENGTH, rawMessage.length(),
                    rawMessage));
        }

        String rawId = rawMessage.substring(0, Transmission.ID_LENGTH);
        String rawContent = rawMessage.substring(Transmission.ID_LENGTH);
        try {
            int id = Integer.parseInt(rawId);
            String content = rawContent.trim();
            return new Transmission(id, content);
        } catch (NumberFormatException e) {
            throw new IllegalArgumentException(
                String.format("Expected number, but got '%s' in '%s'",
                    rawId, rawMessage));
        }
    }
}
```

Instead of missing or useless information, we provide a triplet: what we expect, what we got, and the overall context. A developer who traces an exception to its origin will find the source much faster with such detailed information.

What's more, we can reproduce the situation that causes the exception more easily. Even better, we can reuse such triples as test cases—we just need to convert them into JUnit tests to drive a bug fix and act as regression tests later on. We'll get to testing in the next chapter.

You probably already noticed: we use a template for the message of an exception with *Favor Format Over Concatenation,* on page 32 in the form of Expected [EXPECTED], but got [ACTUAL] in [CONTEXT]. It forces us to include information about what was expected (e.g., 140 characters) and what we got (e.g., 3 characters) and provides the context (e.g., message "abc"). For instance: Expected 140, but got 3 characters in message 'abc'. You can use any format you like, of course. For us, this one really pays off—when (not if) exceptions occur in production.

But we're not done yet. Sometimes, exceptions can't be handled directly. Instead, you have to rethrow or convert them into a more general exception type. When you do, stay clear of the pitfalls we'll explain in the next comparison: *Avoid Breaking the Cause Chain,* on page 80.

Avoid Breaking the Cause Chain

```java
class TransmissionParser {
    static Transmission parse(String rawMessage) {
        if (rawMessage != null
                && rawMessage.length() != Transmission.MESSAGE_LENGTH) {
            throw new IllegalArgumentException(
                String.format("Expected %d, but got %d characters in '%s'",
                        Transmission.MESSAGE_LENGTH, rawMessage.length(),
                        rawMessage));
        }

        String rawId = rawMessage.substring(0, Transmission.ID_LENGTH);
        String rawContent = rawMessage.substring(Transmission.ID_LENGTH);
        try {
            int id = Integer.parseInt(rawId);
            String content = rawContent.trim();
            return new Transmission(id, content);
        } catch (NumberFormatException e) {
            throw new IllegalArgumentException(
                String.format("Expected number, but got '%s' in '%s'",
                        rawId, rawMessage));
        }
    }
}
```

Exceptions can cause more exceptions. When an exception is caught but cannot be handled, it must be rethrown. If a bug is involved, this can propagate until the program crashes. If the error handling was done right, you will be presented with a stack trace that represents the cause chain—a list where each exception is linked to the one that caused it. When tracking down a bug, a detailed cause chain is worth a pile of gold.

That's why you need to make sure that you never break this chain. For instance, look at the code above. It catches the NumberFormatException and throws a new IllegalArgumentException with an informative message instead. No bad exception handling as such—but it breaks the cause chain!

Can you spot the problem? It's the IllegalArgumentException not getting the reference to its cause, the NumberFormatException. Without this link there's no cause chain. When you look at the stack trace of this IllegalArgumentException, you won't find a hint that it stems from a NumberFormatException or from what line in the code. We lost a lot of useful information—the NumberFormatException has its own message that provides more information and context on another level of abstraction and its own stack trace with line numbers.

So how can we keep the cause chain instead of breaking it?

```java
class TransmissionParser {
    static Transmission parse(String rawMessage) {
        if (rawMessage != null
                && rawMessage.length() != Transmission.MESSAGE_LENGTH) {
            throw new IllegalArgumentException(
                String.format("Expected %d, but got %d characters in '%s'",
                        Transmission.MESSAGE_LENGTH, rawMessage.length(),
                        rawMessage));
        }

        String rawId = rawMessage.substring(0, Transmission.ID_LENGTH);
        String rawContent = rawMessage.substring(Transmission.ID_LENGTH);
        try {
            int id = Integer.parseInt(rawId);
            String content = rawContent.trim();
            return new Transmission(id, content);
        } catch (NumberFormatException e) {
            throw new IllegalArgumentException(
                String.format("Expected number, but got '%s' in '%s'",
                    rawId, rawMessage), e);
        }
    }
}
```

Exceptions have various constructors and some of them allow us to pass in a Throwable as a cause. By passing in a Throwable, we link an exception to its cause, thereby building the cause chain. We recommend that you use the constructor Exception(String message, Throwable cause) and provide a message as well.

We've seen many kinds of broken cause chains in actual code. Take a look at the worst of all:

```java
} catch (NumberFormatException e) {
    // BAD! Cause chain interrupted!
    throw new IllegalArgumentException(e.getCause());
}
```

It seems okay. The throw provides e.getCause() as an input parameter and creates a cause chain, but it removes one exception from it, namely the NumberFormatException because it only links *its cause, but not the exception itself.* That's worse than no cause chain, because leaving out selected parts can mislead you.

So if you need to throw an exception within a catch block, just pass in a message and the caught exception as a cause directly:

```java
throw new IllegalArgumentException("Message", e);
```

Expose Cause in Variable

```
class TransmissionParser {
    static Transmission parse(String rawMessage) {
        if (rawMessage != null
                && rawMessage.length() != Transmission.MESSAGE_LENGTH) {
            throw new IllegalArgumentException(
                String.format("Expected %d, but got %d characters in '%s'",
                    Transmission.MESSAGE_LENGTH, rawMessage.length(),
                    rawMessage));
        }

        String rawId = rawMessage.substring(0, Transmission.ID_LENGTH);
        String rawContent = rawMessage.substring(Transmission.ID_LENGTH);
        try {
            int id = Integer.parseInt(rawId);
            String content = rawContent.trim();
            return new Transmission(id, content);
        } catch (NumberFormatException e) {
            throw new IllegalArgumentException(
                String.format("Expected number, but got '%s' in '%s'",
                    rawId, rawMessage), e);
        }
    }
}
```

We sometimes forget that exceptions are also simply classes that can have their own fields, methods, and constructors—not just the standard ones. And we can use them to expose the cause of an exception in a machine-readable way.

In the code above, you can spot two issues: there's duplicate code and concealed information.

The code duplication is where we add rawMessage to the message of the IllegalArgumentException twice in the same way: " in '%s'". This can quickly get inconsistent the larger the software grows.

Concealed information is even more problematic. We encode the rawMessage within the message of the exception. This element can't be extracted easily later on when, for instance, we want to inform the end user of our software what kind of message caused an error. It's concealed from any further processing. And we can also easily forget to add it to the exception message.

So how can we make the context of the exception easier to inspect?

```
class TransmissionParser {
    static Transmission parse(String rawMessage) {
        if (rawMessage != null
                && rawMessage.length() != Transmission.MESSAGE_LENGTH) {
            throw new MalformedMessageException(
                String.format("Expected %d, but got %d characters",
                    Transmission.MESSAGE_LENGTH, rawMessage.length()),
                    rawMessage);
        }

        String rawId = rawMessage.substring(0, Transmission.ID_LENGTH);
        String rawContent = rawMessage.substring(Transmission.ID_LENGTH);
        try {
            int id = Integer.parseInt(rawId);
            String content = rawContent.trim();
            return new Transmission(id, content);
        } catch (NumberFormatException e) {
            throw new MalformedMessageException(
                String.format("Expected number, but got '%s'", rawId),
                rawMessage, e);
        }
    }
}
final class MalformedMessageException extends IllegalArgumentException {
    final String raw;

    MalformedMessageException(String message, String raw) {
        super(String.format("%s in '%s'", message, raw));
        this.raw = raw;
    }
    MalformedMessageException(String message, String raw, Throwable cause) {
        super(String.format("%s in '%s'", message, raw), cause);
        this.raw = raw;
    }
}
```

We suggest that you define and use a custom exception: the MalformedMessage-Exception with its own raw message field. We can obtain that field later on for more detailed end-user information or for a more thorough handling of that exception.

The message still adheres to the template introduced in *Explain Cause in Message*, on page 78—the constructor simply appends the raw message. That makes it easier to have a consistent exception message. If we extract the message construction into a separate method, we also get rid of code duplication.

You just need to make sure that your custom exceptions stay immutable, which we do by declaring the class and its fields final.

Always Check Type Before Cast

```
class Network {

    ObjectInputStream inputStream;
    InterCom interCom;

    void listen() throws IOException, ClassNotFoundException {
        while (true) {
            Object signal = inputStream.readObject();
            CrewMessage crewMessage = (CrewMessage) signal;
            interCom.broadcast(crewMessage);
        }
    }
}
```

Sometimes, you have to deal with dynamic object types at runtime. Dynamic objects can come from various sources, typically when serialized Java objects are exchanged through a channel. Before being able to use them in your program, you'll need to explicitly cast them to a type. If you don't do this properly, your program could crash with some kind of a RuntimeException.

In the code above, you can see a class that reads messages from an InputStream by calling its readObject() method. Such streams in Java are very flexible. For example, you can read input from a file or the network. But to make them so flexible, they aren't typed and just provide you with a plain Object. It's your responsibility to turn that into something your program can work with.

You do this with a cast to the type you expect. In the example above, that's (CrewMessage). This will compile just fine and run smoothly as long as the objects in the stream are indeed of that type.

But the party is over when the stream returns a wrong type! The method has no control over which types are actually written into the stream. What if somebody on the other end of the stream inserts a different message type—for example, a ClassifiedMessage? Whatever the reason, you can be sure that at some point, there will be an object that's not a CrewMessage. Then the method, and probably the complete program, will crash with a ClassCastException.

Can you catch this exception? You can, but you shouldn't, as it typically indicates a bug in the code that you can fix. So instead you should repair the code.

Fortunately, all you have to do is a proper type check before the cast:

```
class Network {

    ObjectInputStream inputStream;
    InterCom interCom;

    void listen() throws IOException, ClassNotFoundException {
        while (true) {
            Object signal = inputStream.readObject();
            if (signal instanceof CrewMessage) {
                CrewMessage crewMessage = (CrewMessage) signal;
                interCom.broadcast(crewMessage);
            }
        }
    }
}
```

The code above first stores the result of reading from the stream in a local variable called signal. The variable's type is Object, so this line can't fail because of typing. After all, every non-primitive Java type inherits from Object.

Next, we make sure that we can read the signal by performing a type check using the instanceof operator. This operator returns true if signal can be cast to the type CrewMessage and false otherwise. We're allowed to do the explicit cast only if the check was positive. It gives us certainty that a ClassCastException won't happen here. We're safe!

This requires additional lines of code, but there's no other way to avoid a ClassCastException in Java. When you expect a set of different types—different types of messages in our example—you'll have to do a sequence of checks with instanceof.

There's another exception type in the method signature that you shouldn't confuse with the ClassCastException. An ObjectInputStream triggers a ClassNotFoundException exception when it tries to read an object whose type isn't in your program's classpath. You can't avoid that with a type check, obviously. Usually, this exception means that there's something wrong in your execution setup, but it shouldn't necessarily stem from a bug in your code. In production, you should also catch and log it. During development, it's better to let the program crash and update the environment before continuing.

So keep in mind that whenever your program interacts with the outside (for example, using a stream), you need to make sure that it can handle unexpected input.

Always Close Resources

```java
class Logbook {

    static final Path LOG_FOLDER = Paths.get("/var/log");
    static final String FILE_FILTER = "*.log";

    List<Path> getLogs() throws IOException {
        List<Path> result = new ArrayList<>();

        DirectoryStream<Path> directoryStream =
                Files.newDirectoryStream(LOG_FOLDER, FILE_FILTER);
        for (Path logFile : directoryStream) {
            result.add(logFile);
        }
        directoryStream.close();

        return result;
    }
}
```

Programs need system resources, such as disk space, database or network connections, CPU threads, and RAM. These resources are limited, and programs have to share them among each other. If a single program acquires resources without releasing them, it can bring down the whole environment. For a more in-depth explanation of this problem, take a look at this article.[2]

We the programmers need to prevent this! The plan sounds straightforward: free resources immediately when they're no longer needed. But as always, the devil is in the details (or rather in the code).

Take a look at the method above. It uses a DirectoryStream, which is a system resource. It frees the resource by calling its close() method. Everything looks correct, doesn't it?

Unfortunately not. When everything goes fine, the program opens the resource, uses it, and then closes it via the close() method. But what if the program opens the resource and an exception occurs while it's using it, before it can free the resource by calling close()? An exception would prevent the execution of close(). Then, the resource wouldn't be freed before the program terminates.

This is called a "resource leak." It can harm the program itself if it tries to acquire the same resource again at a later time. And it's definitely not the way to build a long-running application.

---

2. http://www.oracle.com/technetwork/articles/java/trywithresources-401775.html

So how can we make sure that our code *always* closes its used resources?

```java
class Logbook {

    static final Path LOG_FOLDER = Paths.get("/var/log");
    static final String FILE_FILTER = "*.log";

    List<Path> getLogs() throws IOException {
        List<Path> result = new ArrayList<>();

        try (DirectoryStream<Path> directoryStream =
                    Files.newDirectoryStream(LOG_FOLDER, FILE_FILTER)) {
            for (Path logFile : directoryStream) {
                result.add(logFile);
            }
        }

        return result;
    }
}
```

Since Java 7, we can safely and elegantly close resources with the *try-with-resources* construct. This works for any class that implements the AutoCloseable interface, which practically all resource classes of the Java API do. We need to open only the resource within the round brackets following the try. Then, the resource is available in the scope of the try and Java takes care of calling close() when the block is finished, no matter what.

Actually, the try-with-resources is just syntactic sugar. The compiler expands it into something like this:

```java
DirectoryStream<Path> resource =
        Files.newDirectoryStream(LOG_FOLDER, FILE_FILTER);
try {
    // usage of resource
} finally {
    if (resource != null) {
        resource.close();
    }
}
```

That code opens the resource before the try and uses the finally block to ensure that the resource gets closed for normal and erroneous execution, but only when it's not null to avoid a NullPointerException in the next line. This is clearly not as elegant and simple as try-with-resources.

You don't really need the compiler here—you can implement resource closing on your own. In fact, before Java 7, that's exactly what you had to do. But our advice is: let *your* code be elegant and let the compiler do the *dirty* work.

Always Close Multiple Resources

```
class Logbook {

    static final Path LOG_FOLDER = Paths.get("/var/log");
    static final Path STATISTICS_CSV = LOG_FOLDER.resolve("stats.csv");
    static final String FILE_FILTER = "*.log";

    void createStatistics() throws IOException {
        DirectoryStream<Path> directoryStream =
                Files.newDirectoryStream(LOG_FOLDER, FILE_FILTER);
        BufferedWriter writer =
                Files.newBufferedWriter(STATISTICS_CSV);

        try {
            for (Path logFile : directoryStream) {
                final String csvLine = String.format("%s,%d,%s",
                        logFile,
                        Files.size(logFile),
                        Files.getLastModifiedTime(logFile));
                writer.write(csvLine);
                writer.newLine();
            }
        } finally {
            directoryStream.close();
            writer.close();
        }
    }
}
```

As you've seen before, properly closing resources is important to the stability of your program. If you use many resources at the same time, closing becomes extra difficult.

Always closing *multiple* resources is prone to mistakes, because each resource might fail in some way. That's hard when you close resources manually without a try-with-resources construct.

Let's look at the code above. It uses two resources: a DirectoryStream and a BufferedWriter. That's something you see often: reading from one resource and writing to another.

The resources are opened before the try and closed in the finally block afterward. It looks almost like the manual solution in *Always Close Resources*, on page 86. But exceptions can throw you a spanner here, too:

- If the creation of writer fails, the method will exit with an exception and directoryStream won't be closed.

- If closing directoryStream causes an exception, then writer won't be closed.

We can use try-with-resources again.

```java
class Logbook {

    static final Path LOG_FOLDER = Paths.get("/var/log");
    static final Path STATISTICS_CSV = LOG_FOLDER.resolve("stats.csv");
    static final String FILE_FILTER = "*.log";

    void createStatistics() throws IOException {
        try (DirectoryStream<Path> directoryStream =
                        Files.newDirectoryStream(LOG_FOLDER, FILE_FILTER);
             BufferedWriter writer =
                        Files.newBufferedWriter(STATISTICS_CSV)) {
            for (Path logFile : directoryStream) {
                String csvLine = String.format("%s,%d,%s",
                        logFile,
                        Files.size(logFile),
                        Files.getLastModifiedTime(logFile));
                writer.write(csvLine);
                writer.newLine();
            }
        }
    }
}
```

A try-with-resources block isn't limited to one resource—it can handle multiple resources at the same time. Even when something goes wrong, it ensures that all of the resources are always closed. To use multiple resources in a try-with-resources, you just need to separate them by a semicolon:

```java
try (open resource1; open resource2) {
    // use   resources
}
```

Internally, the compiler expands each resource in the try-with-resources block and creates a nesting of multiple blocks. The innermost try-finally block uses the opened resources.

```java
// open resource1
try {
    // open resource2
    try {
        // use resource1 and resource2
    } finally { resource2.close(); }
} finally { resource1.close(); }
```

Heed our advice: don't manage resources manually—you'll only shoot yourself in the foot. Open resources in a try-with-resources block—and your feet stay unharmed.

Explain Empty Catch

```
class Logbook {

    static final Path LOG_FOLDER = Paths.get("/var/log");
    static final String FILE_FILTER = "*.log";

    List<Path> getLogs() throws IOException {
        List<Path> result = new ArrayList<>();

        try (DirectoryStream<Path> directoryStream =
                    Files.newDirectoryStream(LOG_FOLDER, FILE_FILTER)) {
            for (Path logFile : directoryStream) {
                result.add(logFile);
            }
        } catch (NotDirectoryException e) {

        }

        return result;
    }
}
```

In the last comparison of this chapter, we're going back to catching exceptions. Above, you can see a different version of the LogBook example from the previous pages. It closes resources properly, but something else is strange: the catch block.

You should catch exceptions if and only if you can handle them in a meaningful way. The catch block contains the code that handles the exception. You can handle exceptions in many ways. For example, you can retry something else or just log that the exception occurred.

Sometimes, swallowing an exception and doing nothing is actually the right thing to do. Nevertheless, when we stumble upon an empty catch block, we always get a weird feeling: Is this a bug? Was the catch added unintentionally, for example by the IDE, and does it hide the exception? Or is it a feature? Did the programmer leave the catch block empty on intention?

In the end, we don't know. An empty catch without any hint of why it's empty always looks like a bug. We can't know for sure that it's been intended. That means we'll have to waste precious programming time to double-check.

After all, better to be safe than sorry.

So how can we explain the intentions here?

```java
class Logbook {

    static final Path LOG_FOLDER = Paths.get("/var/log");
    static final String FILE_FILTER = "*.log";

    List<Path> getLogs() throws IOException {
        List<Path> result = new ArrayList<>();

        try (DirectoryStream<Path> directoryStream =
                    Files.newDirectoryStream(LOG_FOLDER, FILE_FILTER)) {
            for (Path logFile : directoryStream) {
                result.add(logFile);
            }
        } catch (NotDirectoryException ignored) {
            // No directory -> no logs!
        }

        return result;
    }
}
```

This looks much better. The catch block no longer signals to us that something might be wrong.

We achieved this with two changes.

First, we renamed the exception variable e to ignored. It's more self-explanatory and states explicitly that we *want* to ignore the exception. This name is almost a convention. Modern IDEs understand it, too, and no longer warn that there's an empty catch block.

And second, we add a comment *why* we ignore the exception. This is important, because others programmers will have it easier to comprehend this decision. Since it's a sort of design decision, we suggest that you use a template here, similar to *Document Implementation Decisions*, on page 46. The template we propose is CONDITION -> EFFECT. The condition captures the reason why the exception has been thrown and the effect states why we can swallow and ignore it.

You might say that the comment alone should be enough. But we recommend that you do the renaming and add the comment. Ultimately, the exception variable always needs a name and we should give it a better one than the generic e.

What Have You Learned?

Handling exceptions is inevitable in any program you write. As you've seen in this chapter, it's easy to get a subtle detail wrong with exceptions, such as forgetting to link exceptions into a cause chain or failing to close resources properly.

When you make such mistakes, your program will still compile. Java doesn't force you to provide good messages for exceptions or to link them with each other. That's a problem, because you might realize these issues only at a late stage, typically when your program has been deployed to production with real-world data. Then, you get bug reports with broken stack traces or meaningless error messages, which makes it very hard to track down their cause. So make your future working life easier by writing proper exception handling code right from the start! It will make a bad impression when you're trying to deploy software at a customer and you can't figure out what's causing the troubles.

That's why we've shown you how to write informative messages for exceptions that help with debugging and how you can expose this information in your program. You're also aware of the things that can go wrong when you deal with exceptions in the wrong way—so you won't accidentally swallow exceptions by catching a type that's too general, forget to check types before casting with the instanceof operator, or create memory leaks by failing to close resources properly. Lastly, we've shown you how to structure your exception handling code in a way that's easier to read and understand: by failing fast and explaining empty catch blocks.

Much of this chapter has been about making sure that your program works even if something goes wrong. After all, some aspects such as file handling or networking are out of your control and you can't prevent such errors from happening. But there are plenty of problems that you can and should avoid. Your program shouldn't contain programming errors, and it shouldn't contain bugs that you could've fixed on your side.

That's easier said than done, but there's one technique that is your first and foremost tool when it comes to making sure that your programming is functionally correct: unit testing. This is the topic of the next chapter. We'll show you how to write high-quality testing code that doesn't just spot bugs, but that lives up to the same quality as your regular code. Don't miss that!

Test your code, or your users will.
> *Dave Thomas and Andrew Hunt*

CHAPTER 6

Assert Things Going Right

To err is human. Or to put it differently, we all make mistakes. No matter how brilliant, how well educated, or how experienced you are, you're still going to write buggy code now and then. NASA's own bugs made its Mars robots land too hard, and its rockets accelerated too fast during takeoff. Pac-Man ended at a kill screen at level 256. And some really terrible software errors have hurt or even killed people—for example, an X-ray machine that emitted too much radiation.

Of course you're going to try to make your software as bug-free as possible. And testing is one technique you'll use for finding flaws. It's not perfect—no amount of testing will ever guarantee you no errors. But that's no excuse for not writing tests at all. You can come a long way with a few very simple techniques that we're going to show you in this chapter.

Luckily, we have decent support for writing tests today—automated tests that you can run for every code change, no matter how small, to make sure that a feature that once worked doesn't break. Java doesn't have built-in testing support, but it has something that comes very close: the JUnit[1] framework. This is the de facto Java standard for automating test execution. Because it's so important, we'll assume that you're familiar with JUnit on a basic level for the following comparisons. You should at least be able to run a JUnit test.

Even if you know how to use JUnit, writing a *good* test suite for the first time is challenging. You need to design test cases appropriately, name them, and use the JUnit API with all its classes, methods, and annotations. This chapter will show you how to *detect* common issues in test cases, and how to *improve* them. We'll go over how to structure a test, describe it, and make it stand alone so the next developer can understand it more quickly in isolation.

---

1.   http://junit.org/

Structure Tests Into Given-When-Then

```
class CruiseControlTest {

    @Test
    void setPlanetarySpeedIs7667() {
        CruiseControl cruiseControl = new CruiseControl();
        cruiseControl.setPreset(SpeedPreset.PLANETARY_SPEED);
        Assertions.assertTrue(7667 == cruiseControl.getTargetSpeedKmh());
    }
}
```

Above, you can see a simple test written with JUnit5. Although it's not part of the Java class library, JUnit's the de facto standard for writing unit tests in Java and JUnit5 is the newest revision. Defining a test is simple enough, and chances are you're already familiar with it: you just add the @Test annotation to a method and JUnit can execute it as a test.

That test above is worth its money—it runs correctly, and it will detect bugs in the code. And because it's part of an assertion, we don't need to apply *Replace Magic Numbers with Constants*, on page 20 for 7667. The problem is, as we've seen so many times before, it's not as well structured and readable as it could be. Readability is just as important for testing code as it is for source code. After all, test code *is* code. But the test here looks like it was written in a hurry and without due diligence.

Usually, a test consists of three core parts: *given*, *when*, and *then*. Consider the following exemplary test specification:

- *given* a calculator showing the number 2
- *when* adding the number 3
- *then* it should show the number 5.

The *given* part sets the stage for the actual test and captures all prerequisites for executing the functionality we want to test. The *when* part triggers the operation that we actually want to test. And in the *then* part, we assert that the result that the *when* trigger produced is actually what we expect.

You can make your test code much more readable if you make this structure stand out in your code. Can you spot which statement of the test above belongs to which of those three parts? There are three lines and three concepts (given, when, then) to match, so you would think it's straightforward. In that case, you're in for a little surprise.

Here's how you can structure the test to communicate its parts more clearly:

```
class CruiseControlTest {

    @Test
    void setPlanetarySpeedIs7667() {
        CruiseControl cruiseControl = new CruiseControl();

        cruiseControl.setPreset(SpeedPreset.PLANETARY_SPEED);

        Assertions.assertTrue(7667 == cruiseControl.getTargetSpeedKmh());
    }
}
```

There's a lot you can do in terms of readability with only little changes. Formatting with new lines to separate the given-when-then parts is already a big improvement. In a sense, we've just applied *Group with New Lines*, on page 30 to highlight the specific structure of the test.

Thanks to the extra vertical empty lines that split the statements, *given*, *when*, and *then* now directly shine in our faces. This makes it so much clearer. For practice, you can add comments into the test code to make the structure even more obvious. Consider the following:

```
// given
CruiseControl cruiseControl = new CruiseControl();

// when
cruiseControl.setPreset(SpeedPreset.PLANETARY_SPEED);

// then
Assertions.assertTrue(7667 == cruiseControl.getTargetSpeedKmh());
```

When teaching, we sometimes recommend adding these comments as a way for students to get used to structuring tests properly. But when you're used to that structure, the vertical empty lines are more than enough. Frameworks like JGiven[2] make this structure even more explicit.

But there's another problem in the code, as you'll see in the next comparison.

---

2. http://jgiven.org/

Use Meaningful Assertions

```
class CruiseControlTest {

    @Test
    void setPlanetarySpeedIs7667() {
        CruiseControl cruiseControl = new CruiseControl();

        cruiseControl.setPreset(SpeedPreset.PLANETARY_SPEED);

        Assertions.assertTrue(7667 == cruiseControl.getTargetSpeedKmh());
    }
}
```

The most basic assertion you can find in JUnit is assertTrue(). In the end, everything boils down to a Boolean value, whether a condition holds or doesn't. Interpreting Boolean expressions is no problem at all for Java, but you can make the life of your fellow developer a lot easier by writing assertions in a way that's more accessible. And you won't usually do this with assertTrue().

Take a look at the code above. The assertion checks that the value of target-SpeedKmh is identical to 7667. Checking for identity with the == operator is fine here because we compare only primitive types: two ints. With objects, you'd use equals() instead.

The test is functionally correct, but there's a problem that surfaces when the test fails. If that happens, we'll get a stack trace with a java.lang.AssertionError that contains the class and line number of the failed assertion, but without any message. So we only know *which* assertion failed, not *why* it failed.

That message (or rather the lack of one) isn't helpful when you're trying to make sense of what's broken. You're not directed toward the location of a bug. That's because the assertion simply doesn't care that two values are compared with each other—it only cares that some Boolean value should be true but is false. So it's simply not possible to describe the failed assertion in more detail.

So how can we provide more information with the assertion so that we get better error messages?

```java
class CruiseControlTest {

    @Test
    void setPlanetarySpeedIs7667() {
        CruiseControl cruiseControl = new CruiseControl();

        cruiseControl.setPreset(SpeedPreset.PLANETARY_SPEED);

        Assertions.assertEquals(7667, cruiseControl.getTargetSpeedKmh());
    }
}
```

The solution is actually quite simple. We use a different assertion, one that's made for checking if two values are the same: assertEquals(). With this assertion, JUnit can provide a much better error message when the test fails. It'll look like this:

expected: <7667> but was <1337>

That's much more informative. Before, we only knew *that* the test failed. Now, we also know *why* the test fails: we expected the value to be equal to 7667, but actually it was 1337.

We've got to admit that it's also possible to provide a more detailed message with assertTrue(). The big difference is that you have to build this message yourself and feed it into assertTrue(), which will display it in case of failure. That means that you'd have to build a message for every assertTrue() in our code base. It's much better to just use an assertion that does this out of the box, such as assertEquals().

You might have recognized the message format. We used it in a comparison not so long ago: *Explain Cause in Message*, on page 78. Exceptions can be very similar to failing tests in a sense, and the message format is very helpful for a developer to determine *why* something isn't working as expected.

There's much more in JUnit than assertEquals() and assertTrue(). Of course, you can also assertFalse(), assertNotEquals(), and assertSame(). You can check that arrays or data structures are equal (read: hold equal contents) with assertArrayEquals(), assertLinesMatch(), and assertIterableEquals(); that you're able to group multiple assertions together with assertAll(); and that execution time is short enough with assertTimeout(). In any case, you should select the assertion that is the best fit for your test, because this will make for better messages.

Expected Before Actual Value

```
class CruiseControlTest {

    @Test
    void setPlanetarySpeedIs7667() {
        CruiseControl cruiseControl = new CruiseControl();

        cruiseControl.setPreset(SpeedPreset.PLANETARY_SPEED);

        Assertions.assertEquals(cruiseControl.getTargetSpeedKmh(), 7667);
    }
}
```

The test above looks correct, doesn't it? You can see its structuring into different parts, it uses assertEquals() to compare the results, and it has a meaningful name. You need to look closely to find a problem in the code.

It gets more obvious when you run the test and the assertion fails. If that happens, you'll get a message like this one:

expected: <1337> but was <7667>

The message tells you that the two values in the assertEquals() method are different. That's why the test fails as it should. So far so good, but the semantics of the message are wrong. In the test, we expect the number 7667 as the correct result and 1337 is the incorrect result that the cruiseControl returns. But the message tells you that it's the other way around.

The error comes from a mix-up in the arguments to assertEquals()—they're in the wrong order. Unfortunately, Java or JUnit can't provide us with type checking support here. After all, the types of expected and actual values need to be the same. The ordering is a purely semantical problem, and it's easy to get it wrong by accident.

In this simple test, we can quickly determine how the message should be. No real problem here. But think about a more complex invocation of assertEquals() that compares large objects that don't give you such an easy view as the int values here. You'll have a hard time understanding the error, and you might go down the wrong road for debugging the cause of it, simply because you'll assume that the message is correct. At least that's the baseline assumption when you read the message of a failing test, and you'd better make sure that it holds.

It's important to take care of the order of arguments for assertEquals() here:

```
class CruiseControlTest {

    @Test
    void setPlanetarySpeedIs7667() {
        CruiseControl cruiseControl = new CruiseControl();

        cruiseControl.setPreset(SpeedPreset.PLANETARY_SPEED);

        Assertions.assertEquals(7667, cruiseControl.getTargetSpeedKmh());
    }
}
```

As you've probably guessed, the solution is very simple in this case. We just need to switch the two arguments of the assertEquals() method.

The error message for our assertion then turns into:

expected: <7667> but was <1337>

That's much better! Now, the message provides the right information and doesn't mislead you any longer. Our rule of thumb is: think *first* about what you expect.

The hard part isn't fixing the bug; it's avoiding it to begin with. We observed this error a lot in code from Java beginners, and we've also seen it in professional code. Yes, it seems like a minor issue. But clear and descriptive assertion messages are tremendously helpful in times of need (failing tests); you're going to be very thankful for meaningful error messages that lead you toward a fix and not in the opposite direction. We've been very thankful for those messages many times over.

This chapter is also a reminder to expect the unexpected. When something breaks in the code, make sure that you have all the information at hand to get a fast understanding of what the correct behavior should be and what part of the code causes the trouble. Having the right order of arguments is one aspect. Others are using fitting assertions (as in the preceding comparison) and configuring them properly, as you'll learn next: *Use Reasonable Tolerance Values*, on page 100.

Use Reasonable Tolerance Values

```java
class OxygenTankTest {

    @Test
    void testNewTankIsEmpty() {
        OxygenTank tank = OxygenTank.withCapacity(100);
        Assertions.assertEquals(0, tank.getStatus());
    }

    @Test
    void testFilling() {
        OxygenTank tank = OxygenTank.withCapacity(100);

        tank.fill(5.8);
        tank.fill(5.6);

        Assertions.assertEquals(0.114, tank.getStatus());
    }
}
```

Here you can see tests that use floating-point numbers instead of integer values. From the source code alone, the tests seem good. The problem is that they're going to fail, even if the code that's tested is functionally correct.

Can you think of why? Here's a tip: On our machine, the second test fails with the message expected: <0.114> but was <0.11399999999999999>. Obviously, the decimal places aren't what we expected.

The problem here boils down to floating-point arithmetic,[3] the way how decimal numbers are represented with 64 or 32 bits. Java does this according to the *IEEE Standard for Floating-Point Arithmetic (IEEE 754)*. We won't go into the details here, but in a nutshell, it's not possible to represent every floating-point number in a finite number of bits. That's why basically all programming languages, Java included, only approximate floating-point numbers. For example, the decimal number 0.1 easily turns into a close approximation in memory, such as 0.1000000000000000055511151231126. And if you only approximate something, there can be rounding errors.

In the test above, all decimals 5.6, 5.8, and 0.114 are only approximated with a double. Of course, we can specify these numbers directly in code, but as soon they're combined at runtime with arithmetic operations, the result will only be a very close approximation to the expected number. And that's why the assertion above fails.

---

3. If you're interested in a comprehensive explanation, we recommend you read *What Every Computer Scientist Should Know About Floating-Point Arithmetic [Gol91]*.

When you test floating-point computations, you need to specify a precision:

```
class OxygenTankTest {
    static final double TOLERANCE = 0.00001;

    @Test
    void testNewTankIsEmpty() {
        OxygenTank tank = OxygenTank.withCapacity(100);

        Assertions.assertEquals(0, tank.getStatus(), TOLERANCE);
    }

    @Test
    void testFilling() {
        OxygenTank tank = OxygenTank.withCapacity(100);

        tank.fill(5.8);
        tank.fill(5.6);

        Assertions.assertEquals(0.114, tank.getStatus(), TOLERANCE);
    }
}
```

Exact matches aren't reliable with floating-point arithmetic. Instead of pedantically insisting on an exact match, we need to tolerate a little bit of difference between the expected and actual values.

This is easy enough with JUnit. The assertion assertEquals(double expected, double actual, double delta) supports a tolerance value called delta. If you need to be exact up to two decimal places, use a tolerance value of $0.1*10^{-2}=0.001$. Here, we want a precision of four decimal places, resulting in a tolerance value of at least 0.00001.

To sum up, you should be aware of precision and specify an acceptable tolerance level whenever you use assertEquals() with either float or double.

Never Use Floating-Point Arithmetic for Money, Ever!

It seems tempting to use float or double when you have to represent monetary values in your code and that's exactly what beginners usually do. After all, we use money in a floating-point form in our everyday life—for example, by paying $1.99 for a chocolate bar. Floating-point values just seem to be the natural representation for that. Don't ever do this!

Sooner or later, your program will produce wrong calculations because of rounding errors. When it comes to money, even small differences will be noticed. Luckily, the solution is simple: don't store dollars in double values; instead, store cents in long variables or use BigDecimal as most banks and insurance companies do in their Java-based systems.

Let JUnit Handle Exceptions

```java
class LogbookTest {

    @Test
    void readLogbook() {
        Logbook logbook = new Logbook();

        try {
            List<String> entries = logbook.readAllEntries();
            Assertions.assertEquals(13, entries.size());
        } catch (IOException e) {
            Assertions.fail(e.getMessage());
        }
    }

    @Test
    void readLogbookFail() {
        Logbook logbook = new Logbook();

        try {
            logbook.readAllEntries();
            Assertions.fail("read should fail");
        } catch (IOException ignored) {}
    }
}
```

Tests and exceptions often go hand-in-hand. Tests ensure that no exceptions are thrown, or that a particular exception must be thrown.

Let's look at the code. There's two examples of tests that depend on exceptions in different ways. The first one fails if an IOException occurs and the second one succeeds in that case. Here we make the tests fail by executing the fail() assertion. The first test catches the IOException and fails, but it hands over the message of the exception for a better traceability of the failed test. The second test succeeds when the exception occurs. This will take the control flow into the catch block and avoid the call to fail().

These two ways of testing for exceptions work, but they come with some downsides. In the first test, we break the cause chain (and we know we should *Avoid Breaking the Cause Chain*, on page 80, of course). We provide only the message, not the full exception with its stack trace. In the second test, we actually expect the exception to occur, but the code doesn't really tell that story. It's quite clouded because the test depends on avoiding the execution of parts of the code. We could add an assertion like Assertions.assertTrue(true, "expected exception occurred") in the catch block, but that doesn't seem much better.

JUnit has a built-in mechanism to handle exceptions:

```java
class LogbookTest {

    @Test
    void readLogbook() throws IOException {
        Logbook logbook = new Logbook();

        List<String> entries = logbook.readAllEntries();

        Assertions.assertEquals(13, entries.size());
    }

    @Test
    void readLogbookFail() {
        Logbook logbook = new Logbook();

        Executable when = () -> logbook.readAllEntries();

        Assertions.assertThrows(IOException.class, when);
    }
}
```

The first test looks very much like the basic test that it is. Each JUnit test contains the implicit assertion that *no exception occurs*. We don't have to add that assertion explicitly—just let JUnit do its job. This really simplifies the test code, since we can remove the try–catch block and the call to fail() completely. The code reads nicer now, and we don't break the cause chain anymore. Whenever an exception occurs, JUnit will display the complete stack trace on failure.

In the second test, we use assertThrows(). This assertion explicitly marks that we expect a specific kind of exception to be thrown in the test. Looking at the code, you can see that there's no try–catch block anymore and no call to fail().

Instead, everything's handled by assertThrows(). All we need to do is to pass the method that we expect to trigger the exception into the assertion. That's something of type Executable for JUnit5. The traditional way of doing this would be to create an anonymous class (new Executable(){...}). Instead, we'd like to point ahead a little because we already applied *Favor Lambdas Over Anonymous Classes*, on page 130 above as it makes for a much more readable alternative to anonymous classes.

Describe Your Tests

```
class OxygenTankTest {
    static final double PERMILLE = 0.001;

    @Test
    @Disabled
    void testFill() {
        OxygenTank smallTank = OxygenTank.withCapacity(50);

        smallTank.fill(22);

        Assertions.assertEquals(0.44, smallTank.getStatus(), PERMILLE);
    }

    @Test
    private void testFill2() {
        OxygenTank bigTank = OxygenTank.withCapacity(10_000);
        bigTank.fill(5344.0);

        Executable when = () -> bigTank.fill(6000);

        Assertions.assertThrows(IllegalArgumentException.class, when);
    }
}
```

Eventually, tests will fail. That's what they're there for—telling you when you break something. When tests fail, the first thing you'll see is their name. Good names are valuable—they help you find the cause for failure faster.

In the code above, we've already done a lot of good things: we've applied *Structure Tests Into Given-When-Then*, on page 94 and the previous comparisons. We even use the assertThrows() assertion that expects a specific exception to be thrown within an Executable. But the code still lacks something crucial: good names and documentation. What do the tests actually check for?

A failing test initially only shows us the class name and the name of its methods. We know that this class contains tests for the OxygenTank class because it follows the [ProductionClass]Test name convention. This is helpful, but the method names aren't; they only list which method is being tested (the method fill()) and a test number. From this name, it's still unclear what they actually test for (except that they test the method fill()). Sadly, you'll find test names like these frequently in real code, because most IDEs automatically generate them using the test[MethodName] convention.

Adding comments might be one option here. But with JUnit5, there are much better solutions.

So how can we improve the test description here?

```java
class OxygenTankTest {
    static final double PERMILLE = 0.001;

    @Test
    @DisplayName("Expect 44% after filling 22l in an empty 50l tank")
    @Disabled("We don't have small tanks anymore! TODO: Adapt for big tanks")
    void fillTank() {
        OxygenTank smallTank = OxygenTank.withCapacity(50);

        smallTank.fill(22);

        Assertions.assertEquals(0.44, smallTank.getStatus(), PERMILLE);
    }

    @Test
    @DisplayName("Fail if fill level > tank capacity")
    void failOverfillTank() {
        OxygenTank bigTank = OxygenTank.withCapacity(10_000);
        bigTank.fill(5344.0);

        Executable when = () -> bigTank.fill(6000);

        Assertions.assertThrows(IllegalArgumentException.class, when);
    }
}
```

The first thing we've done is to get rid of superfluous terms in the method names. They no longer start with words like test. Instead, they describe the context, the method under test, and the assertion we check. The intention in a test named failOverfillTank() is so much clearer than testFill2()! Still, those names have limits: no spaces, and only letters and numbers are allowed.[4]

With JUnit5, there's a solution for adding good test descriptions without tweaking method names: @DisplayName("description with spaces and symbols"). With this annotation, you can use spaces and symbols, such as % or >, to write *really* expressive and compact test descriptions. Spaces make them readable as sentences, and signs allow short and concise descriptions of units.

Describing why a test is disabled is important, because it is your motivation for not just deleting the code. We suggest that you use the format of @Disabled("[why it's disabled] TODO: [what's the plan to enable again]"). This a) forces you to think about the future of this test when you disable it, and b) provides a future developer with the necessary information to enable it again (instead of leaving her high and dry without a clue).

---

4. Since Java 7, you can use any unicode char that passes Character.isJavaIdentifierPart(int). Still, our advice is to stick to digits and letters in method names.

Favor Standalone Tests

```
class OxygenTankTest {
    OxygenTank tank;

    @BeforeEach
    void setUp() {
        tank = OxygenTank.withCapacity(10_000);
        tank.fill(5_000);
    }

    @Test
    void depressurizingEmptiesTank() {
        tank.depressurize();

        Assertions.assertTrue(tank.isEmpty());
    }

    @Test
    void completelyFillTankMustBeFull() {
        tank.fillUp();

        Assertions.assertTrue(tank.isFull());
    }
}
```

When we are teaching Java, we often see beginners who love to use the @BeforeEach and @BeforeAll annotations. After all, they allow you to extract common setup code that you need in the *given* part of a test and write it only once. That's a good thing, because it avoids code duplication. But it comes at a price: setup methods make tests harder to comprehend. Here's why:

In the code above, you can see a setup method (annotated with @BeforeEach) that prepares a half-filled tank and two tests (annotated with @Test) that use that tank. The setup method is at the top of the class, so it's the first thing you read. That placement is fine, but when you read the whole class from top to bottom, you need to recall what it does *for each* single test method. The tests are no longer self-contained.

So what if there are a lot of tests? It's easy to forget in which state the tank is at the beginning. Or what if you're not reading the entire class? Maybe a test just fails at some point. Then you jump directly into the test method and don't find any *given* part there. Instead, you need to scroll around for the setup method. Sometimes, you even have to look up the inheritance hierarchy.

In our code example, it's simple of course. But think about tests in real-world projects with several setup methods spread along the class hierarchy and hundreds of tests. That's a tough one.

The key lies in making the connection of the tests to the setup code clearer:

```
class OxygenTankTest {
    static OxygenTank createHalfFilledTank() {
        OxygenTank tank = OxygenTank.withCapacity(10_000);
        tank.fill(5_000);
        return tank;
    }

    @Test
    void depressurizingEmptiesTank() {
        OxygenTank tank = createHalfFilledTank();

        tank.depressurize();

        Assertions.assertTrue(tank.isEmpty());
    }

    @Test
    void completelyFillTankMustBeFull() {
        OxygenTank tank = createHalfFilledTank();

        tank.fillUp();

        Assertions.assertTrue(tank.isFull());
    }
}
```

Essentially, we've made the tests stand alone. A test stands alone when you link the *given*, *when*, and *then* bits directly within the test method.

Instead of separating the *given* part of the test to the @BeforeEach setup method, we put that part back in each test. Of course, we're not saying you should duplicate code. That's why we extracted the setup part into a static method that we gave a meaningful name: createHalfFilledTank().

Now you can understand each test independently and you don't have to look for setup logic that's implicitly linked elsewhere. It's also easier to move a test from one test class into another, because you no longer have implicit dependencies. The compiler will tell you if you forgot something. That's possible because the test stands alone—all dependencies are explicit.

So in summary: we suggest you avoid the @BeforeEach and @BeforeAll annotations, even though their usage is common. They create implicit dependencies that the framework can easily deal with, but they're making the code less readable for you as a programmer. Tests are better if they stand alone and you can understand the complete test just by looking at the test method and without having to scroll around in the code. If your test setup consists of more than two variables, refrain from falling back to @BeforeEach and create a class for the whole test setup instead.

Parametrize Your Tests

```
class DistanceConversionTest {

    @Test
    void testConversionRoundTrip() {
        assertRoundTrip(1);
        assertRoundTrip(1_000);
        assertRoundTrip(9_999_999);
    }

    private void assertRoundTrip(int kilometers) {
        Distance expectedDistance = new Distance(
                DistanceUnit.KILOMETERS,
                kilometers
        );

        Distance actualDistance = expectedDistance
                .convertTo(DistanceUnit.MILES)
                .convertTo(DistanceUnit.KILOMETERS);

        Assertions.assertEquals(expectedDistance, actualDistance);
    }
}
```

Sometimes, you need to test a method or chain of methods in the same way, but with many different input parameters. That's when you want to make sure that the method works for a large range of values. It's easy to enumerate the parameters in a test method, like in the code above, but this can complicate testing.

The method above tests that you can convert distance values back and forth and get the same result. Can you spot an issue with this method? At a glance, it looks clean and readable. The private method assertRoundTrip() also conforms to our structure of given-when-then.

Think about test execution. What happens if the first assertion, the call to assertRoundTrip(1), already fails? In that case, JUnit marks the complete test as failed and skips the other two assertions with the integers 1000 and 9999999. You'd have to fix the bug that caused assertRoundTrip(1) to fail, run the test again, only to find that now the second assertion, assertRoundTrip(1000), fails as well. Put differently, the assertions hide the ones that follow in the code above.

You can't fix this with a for loop in the test method that iterates over a set of parameters. The only solution is to execute a different test *for every parameter* and have one assertion per test. Adding new test methods is easy, but what if you need tests for thirty different integers here? This would be a lot of code repetition.

Luckily, JUnit has special assertions for exactly this situation:

```
class DistanceConversionTest {

    @ParameterizedTest(name = "#{index}: {0}km == {0}km->mi->km")
    @ValueSource(ints = {1, 1_000, 9_999_999})
    void testConversionRoundTrip(int kilometers) {
        Distance expectedDistance = new Distance(
                DistanceUnit.KILOMETERS,
                kilometers
        );

        Distance actualDistance = expectedDistance
                .convertTo(DistanceUnit.MILES)
                .convertTo(DistanceUnit.KILOMETERS);

        Assertions.assertEquals(expectedDistance, actualDistance);
    }
}
```

The solution here consists of parameterized tests with the @ParameterizedTest and @ValueSource annotations. They allow us to separate the *parameters* (i.e., the input and expected output) from the actual *test code*. Upon execution, JUnit runs a separate test for every parameter.

We declared the parameters in the @ValueSource(ints = { ... }) annotation as an array of integers. Here, we're lucky to have the input match the expected output, due to the roundtrip nature of the test. Sometimes, you just expect that no exception is thrown (see *Let JUnit Handle Exceptions*, on page 102).

We also apply *Describe Your Tests*, on page 104 here, with the name variable inside @ParameterizedTest(name = ""). The variable {index} refers to the index of the test and we can also reference the arguments of the test method with curly braces. {0} stands for the first one and, in this case, the only one. That way, our test description reads like a compressed form of the whole test.

You can inject parameters from different sources such as CSV files, return values of methods, or explicitly in code, as we've done. As a rule of thumb, if you have only a few parameters, it's better to declare them explicitly. CSV files or method return values are better if their amount is very large.

Parameterized tests are only the beginning. Property-based testing libraries such as junit-quickcheck[5] that automatically generate inputs and expected outputs are the next step. With such a technique, it's easy to cover a large range of parameters without having to maintain a large list of parameters in code.

---

5. https://github.com/pholser/junit-quickcheck

Cover the Edge Cases

```
class TransmissionParserTest {

    @Test
    void testValidTransmission() {
        TransmissionParser parser = new TransmissionParser();

        Transmission transmission = parser.parse("032Houston, UFO sighted!");

        Assertions.assertEquals(32, transmission.getId());
        Assertions.assertEquals("Houston, UFO sighted!",
                transmission.getContent());
    }
}
```

In a perfect world, you'd test your code for every possible input parameter. But most of the time, you simply can't. Already, a simple 32-bit integer would require 2^32 tests. That's over 4 billion! Instead of testing every possibility, you should cover the normal execution path and the settings that are most likely to go wrong. Put differently, you should cover edge cases.

The code above contains a single test. It's a test for the normal path—the scenario when a valid input (a String message) produces a typical output (a non-empty Transmission). But what if the input String isn't regular?

- null (null reference)
- "" (the empty String)
- " " (a String with only whitespace characters)
- or "a\nt̂ iŋɑn\nb" (a String with special non-English characters)

You can test for many different versions of a regular input, but the ones above are usually far more likely to uncover a bug in your system.

Edge cases are highly specific for a piece of code, but usually you should at least try the boundaries of a parameter's data type. You've seen String above, and here are some more examples:

- int: 0, 1, -1, Integer.MAX_VALUE, Integer.MIN_VALUE
- double: 0, 1.0, -1.0, Double.MAX_VALUE, Double.MIN_VALUE
- Object[]: null, {}, {null}, {new Object(), null}
- List<Object>: null, Collections.emptyList(), Collections.singletonList(null), Arrays.asList(new Object(), null)

That's a lot, but not all. For example, what are edge cases for email addresses, or uploaded photos? In our example above, which transmission strings are edge cases? Edge cases are the perfect candidate for further tests.

Let's take a look at which edge cases we should cover here:

```java
class TransmissionParserTest {

    @Test
    void testValidTransmission() {
        TransmissionParser parser = new TransmissionParser();

        Transmission transmission = parser.parse("032Houston, UFO sighted!");

        Assertions.assertEquals(32, transmission.getId());
        Assertions.assertEquals("Houston, UFO sighted!",
                transmission.getContent());
    }

    @Test
    void nullShouldThrowIllegalArgumentException() {
        Executable when = () -> new TransmissionParser().parse(null);
        Assertions.assertThrows(IllegalArgumentException.class, when);
    }

    @Test
    void malformedTransmissionShouldThrowIllegalArgumentException() {
        Executable when = () -> new TransmissionParser().parse("tlhIngan");
        Assertions.assertThrows(IllegalArgumentException.class, when);
    }

}
```

We added two new tests: one for null and one for "tlhIngan". In both cases, the parser should respond with an IllegalArgumentException to indicate that the input is invalid. Checking for null is *the* standard edge case with the worst consequences. The other test covers input with a lot of different unicode symbols indicating a malformed string with arbitrary input.[6]

Of course, we could have added a lot of additional tests—for instance, with a message that only slightly deviates from the expected format or where order of the parts in the message is switched. There are no boundaries for your imagination here. But you must be economical when you're testing. Such additional tests are less likely to unveil bugs than the edge cases above. When you stumble upon bugs that aren't covered by the tests, you can still add more tests to ensure that this bug remains fixed.

Edge cases don't necessarily have to be invalid, even if they often are. Sometimes you want to allow special constellations of inputs. In that case, you should still test them to make sure that they actually work.

---

6. Actually, it's Klingon for the word "Klingon." You usually don't have to support that language in your program, but what about languages like Chinese or Turkish? Would your program work with those, too?

What Have You Learned?

You can't have a sophisticated piece of software without testing code. Sometimes (read: quite often), you'll write as much or even more code for testing than you will for implementing the actual functionality. You might even try test-driven development—writing tests before you write the actual source code that's to be tested, and making the tests drive the design of your program. We all know: tests are crucial! That's why you have to make sure that your test suite is well designed and up to the highest standard.

It's important that your tests are concise and to the point. Whenever one of them fails, the code should give you a very clear indication of where to search for the error. Most of the comparisons in this chapter focus on that aspect. We have shown you a template for structuring your tests that consists of *given-when-then* and makes them more understandable. You know that tests should stand on their own, and you learned how you can further improve their understandability by describing them with annotations and choosing the right assertions. You're aware of a few common mistakes people make with JUnit tests—for example, by mixing up expected and actual values or choosing an improper level of precision. Last but not least, you now have a few techniques at hand that will help you to test a lot of your code base while keeping down the amount of testing code. You can get this done by testing the most critical settings, the edge cases, or by parameterizing your tests.

This chapter gave you a first glimpse of what the JUnit framework is capable of. And that's really a lot. In fact, it's capable of much more than we can reasonably cover here—we don't want to write a whole book about unit testing with JUnit. Our aim was just to give you a head start on JUnit with some best practices. Fortunately, that book was already written: *Pragmatic Unit Testing in Java 8 with JUnit [LHT15]*.

Now that you've learned about designing testing code, you're ready for the following chapter—it's high time that we go back to the actual source code and have a closer look at its design. So next, we'll show you a number of design principles that you can apply to make your programs more object-oriented and robust.

Any problem in computer science can be solved with another layer of indirection. But that usually will create another problem.

    David Wheeler

CHAPTER 7

Design Your Objects

Design is something that's important in many disciplines. An architect, for example, can build a house that's fully functional and ready to move into. Roof, windows, electricity, clean water, heating—everything can be in place and working.

Still, you might not want to live there. Maybe it's ugly; neon-painted walls and ceilings shelter you from the rain, but you don't want to stare at those bright colors all the time. Maybe it's inconvenient; a pillar in the center of your living room holds the roof up, but it also keeps you from watching TV from your sofa.

These are exaggerations (hopefully!), but there could be smaller glitches that would annoy you in your new home.

This is where design comes in. Our house shouldn't just be functional. We want the architect to make it beautiful and convenient, too. The same applies to our classes and objects in Java. They shouldn't just be functionally correct. They should be beautiful to look at, and they should be convenient to use.

There are many little tricks that an architect can apply while designing a house. They might be so small that you don't even notice that there's a design rationale behind them. It's the same with object-oriented design in Java. There are many little tricks you can apply to design your program.

These tricks (read: best practices) are what this chapter is about. We'll highlight some of Java's most common design principles that help you to produce code that's more object-oriented (beautiful) and robust (convenient).

The best practices you'll learn in this chapter aren't just relevant when you write the code the first time. They'll help you to improve existing code—for example, when you have to put a system under test.

Split Method with Boolean Parameters

```java
class Logbook {

    static final Path CAPTAIN_LOG = Paths.get("/var/log/captain.log");
    static final Path CREW_LOG = Paths.get("/var/log/crew.log");

    void log(String message, boolean classified) throws IOException {
        if (classified) {
            writeMessage(message, CAPTAIN_LOG);
        } else {
            writeMessage(message, CREW_LOG);
        }
    }

    void writeMessage(String message, Path location) throws IOException {
        String entry = LocalDate.now() + " " + message;
        Files.write(location, Collections.singleton(entry),
                StandardCharsets.UTF_8, StandardOpenOption.APPEND);
    }
}
```

In general, a method should specialize on a single task only. Boolean method parameters show that a method does at least two things.

In this example, we're revisiting a refined version of the Logbook class. We separate messages into classified and non-classified messages via a boolean parameter of the log() method. Here's a usage example:

```java
logbook.log("Aliens sighted!", true);
logbook.log("Toilet broken.", false);
```

This code doesn't contain a bug, but it's less readable and structured than it should be. Everybody who reads it will have to figure out what purpose that boolean parameter serves. If people can figure out the purpose, there's still a risk that they'll interpret it the wrong way and write a classified message in the crew log.

Using a boolean value as a method parameter helps you loudly to proclaim that the method does more than one thing. This is sometimes okay, but it generally makes your code less understandable because it's hard to see on the calling side what the boolean parameter actually achieves. Furthermore, the two logs are coupled. If you want to make a change in the logic of the captain's log, you risk that the changes affect the crew log, since they are handled in the same method. That's nothing you want to have, right?

Check out how we can improve this:

```
class Logbook {

    static final Path CAPTAIN_LOG = Paths.get("/var/log/captain.log");
    static final Path CREW_LOG = Paths.get("/var/log/crew.log");

➤   void writeToCaptainLog(String message) throws IOException {
        writeMessage(message, CAPTAIN_LOG);
    }

➤   void writeToCrewLog(String message) throws IOException {
        writeMessage(message, CREW_LOG);
    }

    void writeMessage(String message, Path location) throws IOException {
        String entry = LocalDate.now() + " " + message;
        Files.write(location, Collections.singleton(entry),
                StandardCharsets.UTF_8, StandardOpenOption.APPEND);
    }
}
```

Whenever you see a method that uses a boolean input parameter, chances are that you can improve the code by separating it into multiple methods.

To do so, you remove the boolean method parameter and add a new method for each control-flow path that the parameter was distinguishing between. You can even give the new methods expressive and meaningful names and further enhance the readability of the code!

This is also what we've done in the code above: we've added the two new methods writeToCaptianLog() and writeToCrewLog(). Consider the new usage now:

```
logbook.writeToCaptainLog("Aliens sighted!");
logbook.writeToCrewLog("Toilet broken. Again...");
```

As you can see, this is much more readable than the previous version. The method names make it clear which log a message belongs to, and you can tell from the calling code what the method is intended to achieve.

Remember: Good Design Is Difficult

Hardly anybody gets it right on their first try. In the end, this is good news because it means that your skills will be in high demand when you master object-oriented design. But be aware that it's harder to tell good from bad design than it is to spot a botched line of code. Good design is less clear-cut, and it requires you to have an intuition and a "feeling" for it. The only real way to get this intuition is to do a lot of coding, to try out different designs, and to see what fails and what feels just right.

Split Method with Optional Parameters

```
class Logbook {

    static final Path CREW_LOG = Paths.get("/var/log/crew.log");

    List<String> readEntries(LocalDate date) throws IOException {
        final List<String> entries = Files.readAllLines(CREW_LOG,
                StandardCharsets.UTF_8);
        if (date == null) {
            return entries;
        }

        List<String> result = new LinkedList<>();
        for (String entry : entries) {
            if (entry.startsWith(date.toString())) {
                result.add(entry);
            }
        }
        return result;
    }
}
```

Booleans as you've seen them in *Split Method with Boolean Parameters*, on page 114 aren't the only indicators of methods that do too much. Optional parameters have the same problem, but they're harder to spot.

This time, we're looking at how data can be read from the log via the method readEntries(). Log entries have a date, and we can select entries marked by the input parameter date. If you insert null instead of a concrete date value, then readEntries() returns all log entries. Consider the following usage:

```
List<String> completeLog = logbook.readEntries(null);

final LocalDate moonLanding = LocalDate.of(1969, Month.JULY, 20);
List<String> moonLandingLog = logbook.readEntries(moonLanding);
```

The semantics of null here essentially mean that the date parameter is optional. This is really just a different version of a boolean method parameter.

As before, a method with optional parameters is a method that does more than one thing. Even worse, it's hard to see what to expect from a method call with a null parameter.

Here's how we can refactor this:

```java
class Logbook {

    static final Path CREW_LOG = Paths.get("/var/log/crew.log");

    List<String> readEntries(LocalDate date) throws IOException {
        Objects.requireNonNull(date);

        List<String> result = new LinkedList<>();
        for (String entry : readAllEntries()) {
            if (entry.startsWith(date.toString())) {
                result.add(entry);
            }
        }
        return result;
    }

    List<String> readAllEntries() throws IOException {
        return Files.readAllLines(CREW_LOG, StandardCharsets.UTF_8);
    }
}
```

The solution to the problem here is essentially the same as in *Split Method with Boolean Parameters*, on page 114: we split the method into two methods. Each of them captures one of the control-flow branches.

In the code above, the readEntries() method no longer permits an optional date parameter and throws a NullPointerException in this case instead. The semantics of the former optional parameter are now captured in the readAllEntries() method, which requires no parameters. This even makes it easier to use. Now the usage looks like this:

```java
List<String> completeLog = logbook.readAllEntries();

final LocalDate moonLanding = LocalDate.of(1969, Month.JULY, 20);
List<String> moonLandingLog = logbook.readEntries(moonLanding);
```

As you can see, this is much more understandable, since the method name clearly communicates that all entries will be read. Apart from getting rid of the null input value, other usages of readEntries() are unchanged.

On top of the improved readability, we're now even avoiding explicit usages of null in our code. The more we get rid of null values, the less likely it is that we'll trigger NullPointerExceptions unintentionally.

Favor Abstract Over Concrete Types

```java
class Inventory {
    LinkedList<Supply> supplies = new LinkedList();

    void stockUp(ArrayList<Supply> delivery) {
        supplies.addAll(delivery);
    }

    LinkedList<Supply> getContaminatedSupplies() {
        LinkedList<Supply> contaminatedSupplies = new LinkedList<>();
        for (Supply supply : supplies) {
            if (supply.isContaminated()) {
                contaminatedSupplies.add(supply);
            }
        }
        return contaminatedSupplies;
    }
}
```

Interfaces and classes often form large type hierarchies—just look at the Java API. If you use more abstract types for variables, your code will be more flexible.

Above, you can see a part of the Inventory system. The method getContaminated-Supplies() loops through a LinkedList of Supply objects, which you can populate via the stockUp() method. Here's how you might use the class:

```java
Stack<Supply> delivery = cargoShip.unload();
ArrayList<Supply> loadableDelivery = new ArrayList<>(delivery);
inventory.stockUp(loadableDelivery);
```

In the example, supplies are delivered in a last-in-first-out (LIFO) order through a Stack. Unfortunately, the Inventory requires an ArrayList for stocking up. So you have to move the supplies into an ArrayList.

Once in the Inventory, the stockUp() method moves the supplies from the ArrayList into an internal LinkedList. From this LinkedList, you can finally extract contaminated supplies via getContaminatedSupplies().

As you can see, there's a lot of conversion between different types of data structures going on, and most of it is actually unnecessary. Plus, changes in Inventory easily propagate elsewhere.

We can get rid of these problems by using more abstract types.

```java
class Inventory {
    List<Supply> supplies = new LinkedList();

    void stockUp(Collection<Supply> delivery) {
        supplies.addAll(delivery);
    }

    List<Supply> getContaminatedSupplies() {
        List<Supply> contaminatedSupplies = new LinkedList<>();
        for (Supply supply : supplies) {
            if (supply.isContaminated()) {
                contaminatedSupplies.add(supply);
            }
        }
        return contaminatedSupplies;
    }
}
```

The solution above differs in three ways.

First, the supplies field uses the interface type List instead of LinkedList. This tells us that the supplies are stored in an order but not how they're stored (in an array for the ArrayList or through linked wrapper objects for the LinkedList).

Second, the method stockUp() accepts any Collection now. This is Java's most general interface for storing objects in a data structure. It means that you can pass any subtype of Collection, any complex data structure in Java, into the method.

Third, the method getContaminatedSupplies() returns a List instead of a more specific type. We guarantee only that the supplies are ordered, but not how the list is implemented internally. This makes the code more flexible.

```java
Stack<Supply> delivery = cargoShip.unload();
inventory.stockUp(delivery);
```

Now, the Inventory accepts the Stack directly without any conversion, because a Stack is a Collection. The Inventory could now handle loading from Sets, Lists, or if need be, even from Vectors and other special-purpose data structures.

Favor Immutable Over Mutable State

```
class Distance {
    DistanceUnit unit;
    double value;

    Distance(DistanceUnit unit, double value) {
        this.unit = unit;
        this.value = value;
    }

    static Distance km(double value) {
        return new Distance(DistanceUnit.KILOMETERS, value);
    }

    void add(Distance distance) {
        distance.convertTo(unit);
        value += distance.value;
    }

    void convertTo(DistanceUnit otherUnit) {
        double conversionRate = unit.getConversionRate(otherUnit);
        unit = otherUnit;
        value = conversionRate * value;
    }
}
```

By default, the state of objects is mutable. Whenever possible, you should make the state immutable because this makes objects harder to misuse.

The code here computes and converts distances for route planning. There's no immediate bug in the code, but the problem is that the Distance class doesn't defend itself from misuse. Consider the following code:

```
Distance toMars = new Distance(DistanceUnit.KILOMETERS, 56_000_000);
Distance marsToVenus = new Distance(DistanceUnit.LIGHTYEARS, 0.000012656528);
Distance toVenusViaMars = toMars;
toVenusViaMars.add(marsToVenus);
```

We first create the distances from Earth to Mars in the variable toMars and from Mars to Venus in the variable marsToVenus. Then we compute the distance from Earth to Venus with a stopover at Mars in the variable toVenusViaMars.

The problem is that toVenus and toMars point to the same object. When we call toVenusViaMars.add(marsToVenus), we're changing the value of toMars indirectly. If we reuse toMars later, we're going to get a false distance value—especially if we pass the toMars instance around in a larger application where any code could alter it.

Let's have the compiler make sure that this can't happen.

```java
final class Distance {
    final DistanceUnit unit;
    final double value;

    Distance(DistanceUnit unit, double value) {
        this.unit = unit;
        this.value = value;
    }

    Distance add(Distance distance) {
        return new Distance(unit, value + distance.convertTo(unit).value);
    }

    Distance convertTo(DistanceUnit otherUnit) {
        double conversionRate = unit.getConversionRate(otherUnit);
        return new Distance(otherUnit, conversionRate * value);
    }
}
```

Objects should defend themselves from invalid changes, and you can achieve this by limiting their mutability.

Note the usage of the final keyword in the code above. Now you need to set the value and unit fields in the constructor, and you can't change them afterward. If you compute a distance, you need a new instance every time:

```java
Distance toMars = new Distance(DistanceUnit.KILOMETERS, 56_000_000);
Distance marsToVenus = new Distance(DistanceUnit.LIGHTYEARS, 0.000012656528);
Distance toVenusViaMars = toMars.add(marsToVenus)
                                .convertTo(DistanceUnit.MILES);
```

As you can see, we can no longer make the mistake we made before. The immutable state of a Distance prevents us from doing so. The downside of this solution is that we create more objects, but in Java small objects are cheap.

In software design, this solution is the way to go for so-called *value objects*[1]: percentages, money, currency, times, dates, coordinates and, of course, distances. These objects are indistinguishable if their values are equal: $10 is $10, even if there's a different object representing each of those dollars. So watch out for *value objects* and make them immutable!

One more note on the final keyword before the class definition: this is required to ensure that this class can't be extended anymore. Doing so would potentially allow us to add mutable state again.

---

1. https://martinfowler.com/bliki/ValueObject.html

Combine State and Behavior

```
class Hull {
    int holes;
}

class HullRepairUnit {

    void repairHole(Hull hull) {
        if (isIntact(hull)) {
            return;
        }
        hull.holes--;
    }

    boolean isIntact(Hull hull) {
        return hull.holes == 0;
    }
}
```

The combination of state and behavior is one of the cornerstones of object-oriented programming. Classes containing only behavior but lacking state indicate OO-design problems.

In the code snippet here, the Hull class captures state and tracks the amount of its holes. The HullRepairUnit can fix those holes, and it captures behavior.

The code above separates state and behavior into two distinct classes. This separation is something you'll find quite often in a beginner's code. Generic examples are a User and a UserController, or an Order and an OrderManager.

The problem is that this separation prohibits information hiding, and it makes the code more verbose. The Hull class has to provide read and (much worse) write access of its state to the HullRepairUnit. It isn't easy to prevent other objects from accessing and modifying the number of holes this way. On top of that, there's also no validation for the hull parameter.

A separation of state and behavior is sometimes hard to detect. As a rule of thumb, you can look out for classes that are simply too large or that operate only on their method parameters. Try to simplify such classes by grouping variables and methods that perform similar tasks into one class each. After that, make sure to do a *before-and-after* comparison to see if you've actually improved the design.

Let's see how we can build a more convincing combination of state and behavior!

```
class Hull {
    int holes;

➤   void repairHole() {
        if (isIntact()) {
            return;
        }
        holes--;
    }

➤   boolean isIntact() {
        return holes == 0;
    }
}
```

The solution above requires substantially less code. The HullRepairUnit is completely gone. Instead, the Hull repairs itself. This may look strange at first, because in reality, there's probably a robot that repairs the Hull. But as long as this unit has no state and behavior in our program, there shouldn't be a class that represents it.

The Hull class can provide the functionality itself instead. Similarly, an Order or User in a different type of system can provide functionality on its own without a manager, controller, service, or any other stateless class.

Generally speaking, we combined state and behavior in this solution. In the problem, they were separated into two classes. In the solution, they're very close to each other, inside the same class. The classes' methods can simply work with the internal state directly. We also reduced the number of method parameters and made the methods easier to understand. Before, parameters had to be validated, but that's no longer necessary. And there's no longer a need to expose the holes attribute to the outside via getters or setters.

To sum up, watch out for methods that only work with their input parameters but not with the instance variables of the class they live in. Those methods indicate a separation of state and behavior and prevent information hiding. With too much information in the open, bugs can easily occur.

Sometimes, frameworks require you to go against this rule. For example, controllers in web frameworks are typically stateless—that is, they have no fields, only method parameters. That's by design to make it possible to create lots of such controllers to handle a large amount of parallel requests—with the state residing in the database only.

Avoid Leaking References

```
class Inventory {

    private final List<Supply> supplies;

    Inventory(List<Supply> supplies) {
        this.supplies = supplies;
    }

    List<Supply> getSupplies() {
        return supplies;
    }
}
```

Practically any nontrivial object has some inner state that's accessible from the outside. You need to be careful how you make this state available. Otherwise, you risk serious bugs.

The Inventory here shows a fairly common example of a class that maintains a data structure. That data structure is initialized externally and inserted into the constructor of the Inventory. Nothing's obviously wrong with the class itself, but let's look at the usage:

```
List<Supply> externalSupplies = new ArrayList<>();
Inventory inventory = new Inventory(externalSupplies);

inventory.getSupplies().size(); // == 0
externalSupplies.add(new Supply("Apple"));
inventory.getSupplies().size(); // == 1

inventory.getSupplies().add(new Supply("Banana"));
inventory.getSupplies().size(); // == 2
```

First, we pass the empty externalSupplies to the new Inventory, and getSupplies() returns an empty list. But the inventory doesn't protect its internal list of supplies. Instead, we can change the state of the inventory by adding a supply to the externalSupplies list or by other change operations on the list returned by getSupplies(). Note that the final keyword for the supplies field doesn't prevent this behavior! And right now, we could also pass null into the constructor, which can easily trigger exceptions later.

The problem is that there's only one list in memory—the one created by new ArrayList<>(). The inventory just stores a reference to that list in its supplies field and returns that reference through getSupplies(). Essentially, the Inventory leaks the reference to its inner structure to the outside through the getter. This is bad! But there's a way to avoid this.

How can we protect the internals of a class from being manipulated after the instantiation?

```java
class Inventory {

    private final List<Supply> supplies;

    Inventory(List<Supply> supplies) {
        this.supplies = new ArrayList<>(supplies);
    }

    List<Supply> getSupplies() {
        return Collections.unmodifiableList(supplies);
    }
}
```

The Inventory does a way better job of protecting its inner structure now. Instead of just using the reference to the list we pass in, it only uses the Supply objects in it to fill an internal ArrayList. It will also trigger an exception immediately if you try to enter null.

What's more, it doesn't expose the internal list through getSupplies() directly, but only after wrapping it as a unmodifiableList(). This ensures read-only access. If a call wants to add an element to the list, we would need to write an explicit method for that.

The instance of the internal ArrayList stays private within the Inventory. Its reference never leaves the class. It's hidden away. Protected. The new usage of the Inventory shows this:

```java
List<Supply> externalSupplies = new ArrayList<>();
Inventory inventory = new Inventory(externalSupplies);

inventory.getSupplies().size(); // == 0
externalSupplies.add(new Supply("Apple"));
inventory.getSupplies().size(); // == 0

// UnsupportedOperationException
inventory.getSupplies().add(new Supply("Banana"));
```

Changing the externalSupplies list or the list returned from getSupplies() has no effect on the internal state of the inventory. Even better, any attempt to modify the list returned by getSupplies() causes an UnsupportedOperationException.

This technique is also called *defensive copying*. Instead of reusing a passed data structure, you make a copy to avoid losing control.

Always remember: It's important to protect both the setter and the getter. And your job gets much easier if you don't allow setters in the first place.

Avoid Returning Null

```
class SpaceNations {

    static List<SpaceNation> nations = Arrays.asList(
            new SpaceNation("US", "United States"),
            new SpaceNation("RU", "Russia")
    );

    static SpaceNation getByCode(String code) {
        for (SpaceNation nation : nations) {
            if (nation.getCode().equals(code)) {
                return nation;
            }
        }
        return null;
    }
}
```

When there's no proper value to return in a method call, some programmers just return null. This can harm the stability of your program!

In the code here, we've modeled the relationship between country codes and country names in the class SpaceNations. The usage is straightforward: you pass a String into the method, and it returns the corresponding SpaceNation instance—or null if the country code is unknown.

```
String us = SpaceNations.getByCode("US").getName();
// -> "United States"
String anguilla = SpaceNations.getByCode("AI").getName();
// -> NullPointerException
```

This is error-prone. As you can see, it's easy to trigger a NullPointerException if you use an unknown country code. Because the method potentially returns null, you have to check the return value explicitly each time. Otherwise, you risk triggering a NullPointerException.

The method is an example for bad design. Even if you document the necessity of checking for null, eventually somebody will forget it and trigger an exception.

If null is bad, what should you return instead?

```java
class SpaceNations {

    /** Null object. */
    static final SpaceNation UNKNOWN_NATION = new SpaceNation("", "");

    static List<SpaceNation> nations = Arrays.asList(
            new SpaceNation("US", "United States"),
            new SpaceNation("RU", "Russia")
    );

    static SpaceNation getByCode(String code) {
        for (SpaceNation nation : nations) {
            if (nation.getCode().equals(code)) {
                return nation;
            }
        }
        return UNKNOWN_NATION;
    }
}
```

One solution would be to throw an exception—for example, an IllegalArgumentException or a NoSuchElementException. This is a strong indication for a problem. You'd have to explicitly deal with it on the calling side.

But in this case, we propose you use the *null object pattern*. Instead of returning null, you return a *null object*, an object that explicitly indicates that it has no real value. Here, this is an UNKNOWN_NATION. That way, you don't disturb the program flow and avoid exceptions:

```java
String us = SpaceNations.getByCode("US").getName(); // -> "United States"
String anguilla = SpaceNations.getByCode("AI").getName(); // -> ""
```

It's still up to the calling side to decide what to do when encountering an UNKNOWN_NATION. The difference is that we now have a choice if we want to ignore the value or throw an exception.

Null objects come in different forms: empty strings, empty collections, or special instantiations of a class, as you can find here. But regardless of their form, they all help to overcome the "billion-dollar mistake": the introduction of the null reference by Tony Hoare![2]

In *Favor Optional Over Null*, on page 142, we'll show you how to force the developer to handle the presence and the absence of that value.

---

2. https://en.wikipedia.org/wiki/Tony_Hoare

What Have You Learned?

Good design is doable, isn't it? It's the little details that improve the overall picture, and the art is to spot the flaws in the class at hand.

You probably didn't write a lot of the code you see on your screen most of the time. So you'll probably have to put some effort into understanding a coder's reasoning behind her design decisions. And you always have a lot of choices to make when you design your code. It's your job to weigh the benefits and concerns that each solution imposes. You have to make an informed decision with trade-offs that affect properties of your code, like readability, testability, maintainability, and performance.

The latter is usually the least concerning, at least at the start. When programming Java, you're usually writing verbose but understandable code—that's in contrast to fiddling around with pointer arithmetic and bit vectors as you'll often see in C and Assembly. This doesn't mean that Java programs are slow. It's just that code understandability matters more than performance at the start. You can always go back and optimize the code later when you've benchmarked it and found a bottleneck. And this is much easier if your code is understandable.

That's what this chapter was all about: improving the understandability of your classes and methods by writing them in a way that makes them intuitive with fewer avenues for misuse. If everybody on the team follows these rules, then development gets easier.

Sometimes you have to split methods and classes into several parts, whereas in other cases you must combine state and behavior. Then there's how you handle references. You shouldn't leak references to internal objects, and it's even better if your objects are fully immutable. This makes them easy to understand, because there can only be one state per object. Finally, a well-designed class is flexible and guides the user to the correct usage. You can achieve this by not returning null references and by using abstract instead of very specific types as input parameters.

The design of large software systems is tremendously hard but it has been explored a lot already. If you want to read more on this, we recommend the classic book on *Design Patterns [GHJV95]*.

In the next chapter, we'll explore a new feature that came with Java 8: functional programming using Java streams and lambda expressions. Streams give you enormous potential for easier data manipulation, faster computations, parallelism, and more stability. So read on!

Object-oriented programming makes code understandable by encapsulating moving parts. Functional programming makes code understandable by minimizing moving parts.

> Michael Feathers

CHAPTER 8

Let Your Data Flow

In the first half of the sixteenth century, the astronomer Nicolaus Copernicus published his ideas on heliocentrism—the astronomical model in which the Earth revolves around the sun and not the other way around. At the time, this was a fundamental revolution of thought and the way that we humans view the universe and our place in it.

The release of Java 8 was a similar revolution to the Java world. Since then, it's become possible to use the functional programming paradigm with lambda expressions and streams in regular Java programs out of the box. Before that, you could only use functional programming on the JVM with different languages like Scala. Now you can combine all major programming styles easily in Java.

Unlike with the astronomic models, there's no right or wrong here. No single programming style describes a fundamental truth. No style is always better than the others in all application scenarios. Each has its pros and cons, and it's up to the developer to find out which suits a particular situation best.

This chapter introduces you to the core concepts of functional programming in Java. We'll go over a number of comparisons that show you when the functional style really tops the imperative one. You'll learn about elegant replacements for anonymous classes, more efficient ways to iterate over data structures, and how to make your program less fragile with Optionals.

But functional programming isn't trivial, and there are a number of pitfalls. That's why we'll explain why you should be very careful with side effects and how you can cope with exceptions in functional programming. You'll see why you shouldn't overuse Optionals, despite their benefits, and how you can switch from the functional style back to the imperative one with the least amount of friction. Let's go!

Favor Lambdas Over Anonymous Classes

```
class Calculator {

    Map<Double, Double> values = new HashMap<>();

    Double square(Double x) {
        Function<Double, Double> squareFunction =
                new Function<Double, Double>() {
                    @Override
                    public Double apply(Double value) {
                        return value * value;
                    }
                };
        return values.computeIfAbsent(x, squareFunction);
    }
}
```

In Java 8, several existing classes (such as Map) got a boost with more useful methods. In the code above, you can see one of them named computeIfAbsent(). This method gets a value from the map using its key, and if the key isn't already present in the map, it computes the value first. Pretty neat. We've written similar code many times by hand before.

But to use that new method, you need to provide the logic, *how* the map should compute the value for an absent key, as an input parameter. Otherwise, it can't do its job.

Type-wise, computeIfAbsent() requires an instance of a class that implements the interface Function<Double, Double> with its method Double apply(Double value) here. The Double types come from the types inside the values map, and you'll have different types for a different map.

In the code above, the programmer instantiated an *anonymous class* to implement that interface. It's called anonymous because there's no class name and the class has only a single instance.

However, anonymous classes have a tendency to bloat up the code. They make it considerably larger and add additional levels of indentation. That's because you need to reiterate the interface type and method. The actual computation—in our example the single line of code return value * value—is hidden in all that verbosity.

With Java 8, we've got an excellent alternative to writing anonymous classes.

Lambda expressions can improve the code a lot here:

```
class Calculator {

    Map<Double, Double> values = new HashMap<>();

    Double square(Double value) {
        Function<Double, Double> squareFunction = factor -> factor * factor;
        return values.computeIfAbsent(value, squareFunction);
    }
}
```

Now that's way shorter and more readable. You can directly spot the computation logic, and all the verbosity is gone for good. Much more concise, indeed.

Lambdas provide implementations for functional interfaces—that is, interfaces with a *single abstract method*. Here, lambdas are a perfect fit, because the Function interface has only a single abstract method: apply(). We can write a lambdas in various ways: as one-liners or in multiple lines. Let's take a look.

```
// one-liner
Function<Double, Double> squareFunction = factor -> factor * factor;
//  multi-liner
Function<Double, Double> squareFunction = factor -> {
    return factor * factor;
};
```

Here, you can compare the one-liner and the multi-liner directly. The one-liner has no return keyword, and no curly braces. It's best for very short and concise glue code. You should avoid the multi-liner whenever possible and *Favor Method References Over Lambdas*, on page 134 instead. And there's more: you can have implicit or explicit type declaration.

```
// without type definition and braces
Function<Double, Double> squareFunction = factor -> factor * factor;
//  with type definition and braces
Function<Double, Double> squareFunction = (Double factor) -> factor * factor;
```

In Java, you usually have to specify types everywhere explicitly. But for parameters of lambda expressions the compiler can figure out the types on its own in (almost) all cases: it searches for the single abstract method that the lambda expression implements and uses that method signature with its type specifications. This is called type inference. We could provide the types here, but why state the obvious?

Note that the braces are only optional for a single parameter and you have to use them for more than one parameter or if the type is stated explicitly.

Favor Functional Over Imperative Style

```java
class Inventory {

    List<Supply> supplies = new ArrayList<>();

    long countDifferentKinds() {
        List<String> names = new ArrayList<>();
        for (Supply supply : supplies) {
            if (supply.isUncontaminated()) {
                String name = supply.getName();
                if (!names.contains(name)) {
                    names.add(name);
                }
            }
        }
        return names.size();
    }
}
```

When it comes to working with collections, a functional programming style can be much more readable than its imperative sibling.

Above, you can see a short but relatively complex method that does some very common things: it iterates over a collection and does a few conditional computations. Even though the code's short and named properly, you need a moment to understand what it's doing.

The code is imperative in style. It tells the computer what to do and how to do it through loops, conditionals, assignments of variables, and method calls. And the machine will simply follow that recipe line by line. You can look over its shoulder with a debugger.

But usually, we're most interested in *what* the code does and not so much in *how* it reaches its goal. That's why we invest so much effort in writing good comments and choosing good names.

Here, the code clouds the intent of the method through its size and the amount of text that we have to read line by line. With lambda expressions, we have the option to specify only *what* we want to get done, without caring about the *how*. That makes for more concise and readable code.

So how can we clarify the code with lambdas?

```java
class Inventory {

    List<Supply> supplies = new ArrayList<>();

    long countDifferentKinds() {
        return supplies.stream()
                        .filter(supply -> supply.isUncontaminated())
                        .map(supply -> supply.getName())
                        .distinct()
                        .count();
    }
}
```

Astonishing, isn't it? Instead of coding the how, we just stated the what, and this makes it so much shorter and more readable. But let's dissect the code line by line.

First, we enter the collection stream(). That's the starting operator, which converts the collection into a stream and opens up the world of functional programming to us! Think of starting a boat rally on a river—each element in the collection is a boat (or use the Collection Pipeline Metaphor[1]).

Second, we filter() out any supplies that are contaminated. A filter is like a gate that allows through only boats that fulfill a condition. Here, the filter only allows uncontaminated supplies to continue their journey. Type-wise, a filter is a Predicate that evaluates something to either true or false—the signature of the single abstract method is boolean test(Supply supply) for this instance.

Third, we transform (or map) our "boats" on the river. You can think of modifying a boat's cargo. In this case, we take out a part of the Supply, its name, and throw the rest overboard. In Java terms, a Function maps a type (Supply) to another one (String).

Fourth, we do more filtering with distinct(): a name is let through only once; any duplicates are discarded.

Finally, we count() the remaining elements in the stream. This is a termination operator that ends the stream and brings us back into the imperative style.

That's still just the surface of what you can do with collections and lambda expressions. The JavaDoc of the java.util.stream package[2] already contains a nicely written guide to the stream API. For a more comprehensive introduction, *Functional Programming in Java [Sub14]* is an excellent reference.

---

1. https://martinfowler.com/articles/collection-pipeline/
2. https://docs.oracle.com/javase/9/docs/api/java/util/stream/package-summary.html#StreamOps

Favor Method References Over Lambdas

```
class Inventory {

    List<Supply> supplies = new ArrayList<>();

    long countDifferentKinds() {
        return supplies.stream()
                    .filter(supply -> !supply.isContaminated())
                    .map(supply -> supply.getName())
                    .distinct()
                    .count();
    }
}
```

Lambda expressions like you've seen them in the previous comparison can make your code more readable. But these benefits come at a price: you can't execute lambda expressions partway—you can only run the whole stream. That means it's hard to test parts of lambda expressions as you'd want to do in a unit test.

Above, you can see a slightly modified solution from the previous comparison: *Favor Functional Over Imperative Style*, on page 132 that uses a logical negation. It contains two lambda expressions, one Predicate to filter and one Function to map. We defined them inline to make the code more concise—they're not referenced by a variable, so we can't use them anywhere else. They're only part of their encompassing method.

You may be wondering: why is this a problem? In very simple cases, it isn't. But if the lambda expressions contains more logic—for example, if the Predicate is a complex condition or the Function a multi-line conversion—then there's potential for errors. And because we can't reference those lambda expressions, we can't test them in isolation with unit tests to ensure that they work as expected. That's not good.

Code that builds on method calls, on the other hand, is easier to test, because you can call the methods separately from their integration. Luckily, functional programming in Java also provides a mechanism to take care of this: *method references*. Using method references, you can embed method calls directly as a lambda expression, and that makes quality assurance easier.

So let's see how can we improve the code with method references:

```
class Inventory {

    List<Supply> supplies = new ArrayList<>();

    long countDifferentKinds() {
        return supplies.stream()
                        .filter(Supply::isUncontaminated)
                        .map(Supply::getName)
                        .distinct()
                        .count();
    }
}
```

The syntax is fairly simple. Instead of defining a normal lambda expression, we can reference existing methods directly in the stream.

Take a look at the code. We've replaced the lambda expressions in the code snippet before, with references to methods. That way, we could even *Avoid Negations*, on page 4! Now, the stream only orchestrates existing (and, of course, tested) methods. This combines the best of both worlds.

And it doesn't stop there: with method references, the code gets shorter and more readable, even if you might have to get used to the syntax at first.

Method references require a special (and new) syntax of the form Class-Name::methodName. For instance, Supply::getName references the getName() method of the class Supply.

Of course, the methods you reference must fit into the place where you use them. The filter operation requires a method reference that fits the Predicate interface (a method that takes an object and returns a Boolean) and the map operation one that fits the Function interface (a method that takes an object and returns an object).

At this point, you might think about converting your lambda expressions into methods. You should do that when the expression is rather complex or when you need it multiple times to avoid "lambda duplication."

As a side note, method references are very flexible: you can even reference a constructor in the form ClassName::new. This may come in handy when turning your stream into a collection with collect(Collectors.toCollection(TreeSet::new)).

Avoid Side Effects

```java
class Inventory {

    List<Supply> supplies = new ArrayList<>();

    long countDifferentKinds() {
        List<String> names = new ArrayList<>();

        Consumer<String> addToNames = name -> names.add(name);

        supplies.stream()
                .filter(Supply::isUncontaminated)
                .map(Supply::getName)
                .distinct()
                .forEach(addToNames);
        return names.size();
    }
}
```

In theory, there are no side effects with functional programming. Everything's just a function that takes data as input and produces new data as output. The data you pass along is immutable.

But in imperative and object-oriented programming, we rely on side effects (we change data and state through procedures or methods) all the time. In Java, we can now mix all these styles. This is very powerful, but it's also quite error prone. That's why you should try to minimize side effects in your code.

Take a look at the code above. It even makes heavy use of side effects to achieve its goal.

The problem is with the Consumer addToNames that's called in the forEach() part of the stream. This Consumer adds an element to a list outside of the lambda expression. That's the side effect.

There's no functional error in the code above, but it's prone to break once you add concurrency. Java makes no guarantees regarding the visibility of side effects among different threads. And already if you parallelize the lambda expression here, it will (occasionally) produce wrong results because the ArrayList is not thread-safe.

Newcomers to functional programming in Java have a tendency to write such code. Whereas the filter() and map() operators only act on the stream elements themselves and don't cause any side effects, beginners often fall back to the imperative style to terminate the stream—and this can only be done through side effects.

So how can we avoid side effects and terminate the lambda expression in a better way?

```
class Inventory {

    List<Supply> supplies = new ArrayList<>();

    long countDifferentKinds() {
        List<String> names = supplies.stream()
                                     .filter(Supply::isUncontaminated)
                                     .map(Supply::getName)
                                     .distinct()
                                     .collect(Collectors.toList());
        return names.size();
    }
}
```

The crucial part is the list that results from the lambda expression. Instead of populating this list ourselves, we collect() every remaining element in the stream in a collection. For a list, you'll need to end the stream with collect(Collectors.toList()). Of course, you can get a Set or other data structures with the Collectors.toSet() as well.

In the example above, we still need to get the size of the resulting list for our job at hand. Let's see if we can do better:

```
return supplies.stream()
               .filter(Supply::isUncontaminated)
               .map(Supply::getName)
               .distinct()
               .count();
```

Yes, we can. The terminating operator count() returns the number of remaining elements in the stream—exactly what we need. It's a shorthand for the reduce operator of the Stream class[3]: reduce(0, (currentResult, streamElement) -> currentResult + 1). This reduces the list to a single integer value. The zero here is the initial value, and we add 1 to the result for every element in the stream.

To sum up, you should try to avoid forEach() for terminating a stream, because it can easily cause side effects. Try to use collect() and reduce() instead, which we'll explain more closely in *Use Collect for Terminating Complex Streams*, on page 138. These operators terminate a stream directly and produce the data structure you need, be it a List, Set, or even a long. This makes your lambda expressions less error prone.

---

3. https://docs.oracle.com/javase/9/docs/api/java/util/stream/Stream.html

Use Collect for Terminating Complex Streams

```java
class Inventory {

    List<Supply> supplies = new ArrayList<>();

    Map<String, Long> countDifferentKinds() {
        Map<String, Long> nameToCount = new HashMap<>();

        Consumer<String> addToNames = name -> {
            if (!nameToCount.containsKey(name)) {
                nameToCount.put(name, 0L);
            }
            nameToCount.put(name, nameToCount.get(name) + 1);
        };

        supplies.stream()
                .filter(Supply::isUncontaminated)
                .map(Supply::getName)
                .forEach(addToNames);
        return nameToCount;
    }
}
```

In the previous comparison *Avoid Side Effects*, on page 136, we showed you how to turn a stream into a single long value with the reduce() operator and its special case, the count() operator. We've also hinted at the collect() operator. This one's best for terminating streams that result in something that's more complex than a primitive value.

Above, you can see slight variation of the code from the previous comparison. Instead of just counting all distinct elements in the supplies list, this code computes how many supplies are available grouped by their name in the form of a Map<String, Long>. If you're a SQL fan, you'll be happy because it's actually quite similar to a SQL query in the form of SELECT name, count(*) FROM supplies GROUP BY name for a table of supplies.

The code contains the same problem as in the previous comparison: we rely on side effects to compute the contents of Map<String, Long> nameToCount. On top of that, the implementation of addToNames is a bit more complicated than the one in *Avoid Side Effects*, on page 136. In practice, such code is almost guaranteed to be even more complex. And the more complex, the harder it is to comprehend.

So how can we rid this complex termination of the stream from side effects and make it easier to comprehend?

```
class Inventory {

    List<Supply> supplies = new ArrayList<>();

    Map<String, Long> countDifferentKinds() {
        return supplies.stream()
                    .filter(Supply::isUncontaminated)
                    .collect(Collectors.groupingBy(Supply::getName,
                            Collectors.counting())
                    );
    }
}
```

If you want to get a Collection as the result of a stream, Java provides you with the collect() operator that we've mentioned in *Avoid Side Effects*, on page 136 and many predefined Collectors that you can use out of the box.

You already know a few of these, like toList(), toSet(), or toMap(). But there are several others, and they're quite powerful.

Consider the code above. First, we use the Collectors.groupingBy() operator on the stream of Supply instances. This operator will always return you a Map data structure.

Here, we want to group the Supply objects by their name. To achieve this, we pass in the method reference Supply::getName. This also specifies the key type of the resulting Map, in our case String. If we used only that, then the expression would return something like a Map<String, Collection<Supply>>. You may have spotted it: we no longer need the map operator here, thanks to groupingBy().

But we don't stop there. The second parameter in our call to groupingBy() is Collectors.counting(). This counts the number of Supply instances within a group. As a result, we get a Map<String, Long> with the number of items per name, as desired.

Take a moment to compare the expressiveness of both solutions. The one using collect() here is much more precise and to the point than the one on the previous page, isn't it? And it reads almost like the highly descriptive SQL query.

And you know what is awesome? There are a lot of additional helpful collectors available, like partitioningBy(), maxBy(), joining(), mapping(), summingInt(), averagingLong(), and, of course, reducing(). In Java 9, you can even use filtering() and flatMapping(), too!

Avoid Exceptions in Streams

```
class LogBooks {

    static List<LogBook> getAll() throws IOException {
        return Files.walk(Paths.get("/var/log"))
                    .filter(Files::isRegularFile)
                    .filter(LogBook::isLogbook)
                    .map(path -> {
                        try {
                            return new LogBook(path);
                        } catch (IOException e) {
                            throw new UncheckedIOException(e);
                        }
                    })
                    .collect(Collectors.toList());
    }
}
```

As you've seen in Chapter 5, *Prepare for Things Going Wrong*, on page 73, you should be prepared for dealing with exceptions. Unfortunately, this can be hard with lambda expressions.

In the code above, we use the Java NIO API to iterate over the filesystem with a stream. Files.walk() opens a Stream<Path> that starts from a given Path and contains all files and directories below that Path.

But when you work with the filesystem, there's always a chance of triggering an IOException. For example, files could be on an external drive that got disconnected, or directories could be deleted by a different process at runtime.

By design streams don't go well with checked exceptions. You have to handle them inside the stream. That's why we catch the IOException in the map() operation and convert it to an UncheckedIOException, which extends RuntimeException.

That's a way to get the whole expression to compile, but it's not beautiful. There's just no proper mechanism to handle exceptions, even unchecked ones, within the functional style in Java. Essentially, this comes from a mismatch of paradigms. Functions work on inputs and produce outputs. Functions don't throw (or catch) exceptions.

Closing I/O Streams

The filesystem is a scarce resource, and you need to take care of closing it properly in your code. *Always Close Resources*, on page 86 springs to your mind. Is that the case here? Well, do you see anything that closes it? We definitely don't.

So how can we deal with exceptions without breaking out of the functional programming style here?

```java
class LogBooks {

    static List<LogBook> getAll() throws IOException {
        try (Stream<Path> stream = Files.walk(Paths.get("/var/log"))) {
            return stream.filter(Files::isRegularFile)
                         .filter(LogBook::isLogbook)
                         .flatMap(path -> {
                             try {
                                 return Stream.of(new LogBook(path));
                             } catch (IOException e) {
                                 return Stream.empty();
                             }
                         })
                         .collect(Collectors.toList());
        }
    }
}
```

As you can see, we still have a try-catch block in the code above. There's no way around this, but we no longer convert the checked exception to an unchecked one. Instead, we simply remove the exceptional element from the stream.

To do so, we used the flatMap() operator. This one's similar to map(), but instead of mapping a type to another one, it maps a type to a Stream of another type. If everything goes right, we simply create a new stream for a single element with Stream.of(element). If there are problems, we just return Stream.empty().

This matches the paradigm of the functional style much better. No matter what, an exception won't take down the entire computation, and the stream produces an output based on its inputs. This also makes reasoning about (and documenting) that code more straightforward. Of course, you can also handle exceptions by logging, but keep in mind that this easily causes side effects, violating the pure functional paradigm.

In a nutshell: You're better off in the functional style if you avoid exceptions.

Closing I/O Streams

We used try-with-resources for the Stream in the code above to make sure that the resource is closed. Admittedly, it does not look as clean as before, but it will do its job. Don't forget this!

Favor Optional Over Null

```
class Communicator {

    Connection connectionToEarth;

    void establishConnection() {
        // used to set connectionToEarth, but may be unreliable
    }

    Connection getConnectionToEarth() {
        return connectionToEarth;
    }
}
```

References that don't point to an object point to the null reference instead. If you try to call a method on a null reference, you cause a NullPointerException. This is probably the most well-known exception in Java.

Using null references is fine for internal state where you have full control over how the reference is accessed. But exposing it makes the program fragile because every caller needs to check for null, which is something that people easily forget. This is what we've discussed in *Avoid Returning Null*, on page 126. But since Java 8 and lambda expressions, we have an alternative to the null object solution.

In the code above, the Connection might not always be available and connection-ToEarth can be null. This can be a problem if the calling code doesn't check for null. Consider the following:

```
communicator.getConnectionToEarth()
            .send("Houston, we got a problem!");
```

This code can trigger the dreaded NullPointerException if there's no connection available.

But it's easy to fix. We just need to add an if statement to check whether the connection we get from calling the getter isn't null.

Still, writing the fix isn't the hard part. That's detecting the issue before that code goes into production. Because you use references everywhere in Java, there's simply too much potential for null references to creep in. Every Java program runs into NullPointerException at some point during development.

What's more, you can't really combine the fix with the if statement with lambda expressions in an elegant way. You'd have to separate the expression into several lines instead. But there's a better solution.

How can we make it explicit that a connectionToEarth might be absent?

```
class Communicator {

    Connection connectionToEarth;

    void establishConnection() {
        // used to set connectionToEarth, but may be unreliable
    }

    Optional<Connection> getConnectionToEarth() {
        return Optional.ofNullable(connectionToEarth);
    }
}
```

With the Optional. An Optional is a placeholder for an object that may or may not be present. You create it by calling Optional.ofNullable() with a reference that may point to an object or to null. Here, a connectionToEarth is either there or it isn't.

The big difference is that you can now spot the potential unavailability in the method signature. Consider the following usage:

```
Connection connection = communicator.getConnectionToEarth()
                                    .orElse(null);
connection.send("Houston, we got a problem!");
```

This reproduces the same behavior as the usage before, including the NullPointerException. But it shows that either we get a Connection object orElse we get null.

Instead of hiding a null value in the Communicator, the Optional reveals it in the caller's code where the access would happen. That way, the Optional forces the caller to think about how to handle an absent value. If you do this as above (orElse(null)), you'll still cause exceptions. So let's fix this here and now:

```
communicationSystem.getConnectionToEarth()
                .ifPresent(connection ->
                    connection.send("Houston, we got a problem!")
                );
```

Without an Optional at hand, we would fix this with an if statement. But the Optional provides a handy method: ifPresent(). This method executes a Consumer you pass in, but only if the value within the Optional isn't null. Here, we simply pass in a Consumer that sends messages. NullPointerException prevented!

A null object for Connection could've solved this, too. But here we resort to a generic null object: Optional.empty(). This saves us development effort, but it's at the expense of having to handle the null object explicitly every time. With lambdas, the Optional class is usually the way to go.

Avoid Optional Fields or Parameters

```
class Communicator {

    Optional<Connection> connectionToEarth;

    void setConnectionToEarth(Optional<Connection> connectionToEarth) {
        this.connectionToEarth = connectionToEarth;
    }
    Optional<Connection> getConnectionToEarth() {
        return connectionToEarth;
    }
}
```

In *Favor Optional Over Null*, on page 142, you've seen that you should rather return Optional values instead of null references. When people learn about Optional, they start to apply it everywhere and for everything. Don't make this mistake! There are situations where Optional can make your code more complicated and inconvenient to use. So let's go over where you should avoid it.

In the code above, we have an Optional field with a setter and getter. From the outside, the code looks nearly identical to the solution in *Favor Optional Over Null*, on page 142. The getter returns an Optional<Connection>. This makes it explicit that the Connection can be absent.

The problem is that the field, connectionToEarth, itself is typed as optional. And there's also a setter that accepts an Optional<Connection>. This introduces more problems than it solves. Can you think why?

We know that an Optional has two states: it's *absent* (or Optional.empty()) or *present*. Those states make sense. But if you have an optional field or method parameter, then this variable can be null as well. So suddenly you have three states: present, absent, or null. What's it supposed to mean if an Optional is null from a semantic point of view? Is it even more absent? That doesn't really make sense. Maybe null in this case means that the current connection should be reset? This isn't clear from the code.

Using optional for typing fields or parameters just makes everything more complicated. We can set fields to null and pass null to methods even with Optional fields or parameters. If you use them, you'll have to check not only for null values, but also whether a value is present.

So what should you do if you encounter Optional fields or parameters?

```
class Communicator {

    Connection connectionToEarth;

    void setConnectionToEarth(Connection connectionToEarth) {
        this.connectionToEarth = Objects.requireNonNull(connectionToEarth);
    }
    Optional<Connection> getConnectionToEarth() {
        return Optional.ofNullable(connectionToEarth);
    }

    void reset() {
        connectionToEarth = null;
    }
}
```

It's relatively straightforward: you should remove the Optional part in the types of fields and method parameters. You should keep the Optional types only as return values. This removes the semantic overload between Optional.empty() and null values.

But if you look at the code above, you can see that it's not as simple as changing types only. When we remove the Optional type of the setter's method parameter, we need to deal with the fact that you can insert null. That was conveniently ignored in the code before. In this case, we check for null values through the useful API method Objects.requireNonNull().

We've also added an additional method, reset(), which gives meaning to a null as prior input parameter. With the reset() method, it's now possible to break the current connection without having to insert an explicit null into the setter. This is more robust and, as you may already have noticed, an application of *Split Method with Optional Parameters*, on page 116. All usages of null references are completely internal to the class, where we have full control on how the field is accessed.

The getter is still the same as in *Favor Optional Over Null*, on page 142. We convert the field into an Optional by calling Optional.ofNullable(). This goes hand in hand with the reset() method, which sets the field to null, because Optional.ofNullable(null) equals Optional.empty().

You might point out now that the getter and setter no longer match the JavaBeans conventions because their types differ. This can be a problem if you have to integrate with frameworks that rely on this convention. In this case, you're forced to make do without Optional return types. Otherwise, Optional can still make your program more robust by avoiding null values.

Use Optionals as Streams

```java
class BackupJob {

    Communicator communicator;
    Storage storage;

    void backupToEarth() {
        Optional<Connection> connectionOptional =
                communicator.getConnectionToEarth();
        if (!connectionOptional.isPresent()) {
            throw new IllegalStateException();
        }

        Connection connection = connectionOptional.get();
        if (!connection.isFree()) {
            throw new IllegalStateException();
        }

        connection.send(storage.getBackup());
    }
}
```

In the previous comparisons, we've shown that Optional can be a good replacement for null. But it's not just that, and there's a good reason why the class was added to lambda expressions in Java. An Optional is also a special kind of stream, one with either zero or exactly one element.

That means that you can directly apply all regular stream operations, such as filter() or map(), to an Optional. This makes for a good opportunity to write more concise code.

Take a look at the code above. It stores a (possibly absent) value in the variable named connectionOptional. That's necessary, because we need to a) check if there's an actual value by calling isPresent(), and b) retrieve that value by calling get(). But it doesn't really make for a good or descriptive variable name.

The reason for storing the Optional in a variable and its awkward name lies in an impedance mismatch. Although this is barely visible in the code, the Optional class is made for the functional programming style, where the rest of the method follows an imperative style. When you switch between these styles, you have to use methods like get() to perform the switch. You can make the code much more readable just by avoiding this context switch.

You'll find such switches very often in code in practice. The functional programming style is still very new for Java. Many developers aren't yet familiar with it, or they have problems applying it fully. That's why they often switch back to an imperative style, even when they started differently.

Check out how much you can improve the code by implementing everything functionally:

```
class BackupJob {

    Communicator communicator;
    Storage storage;

    void backupToEarth() {
        Connection connection = communicator.getConnectionToEarth()
            .filter(Connection::isFree)
            .orElseThrow(IllegalStateException::new);
        connection.send(storage.getBackup());
    }
}
```

It's actually quite simple. Just use the arsenal of methods available in the Optional class: the intermediate operations filter(), map(), and flatMap(), and the terminal operations orElse(), orElseThrow(), orElseGet(), and ifPresent().

In the code above, we used filter() to check if the code is available and free and orElseThrow() to trigger the exception if it's not. That makes for a drastic reduction of the amount of code. Just compare the code listings. In this case, less is more!

The code is way more concise now. And that's not just because we got rid of the strange connectionOptional variable. The code also signals clearly what happens if the connection is absent or not free through the orElseThrow() operation. Before, this was distributed into two separate if conditions.

Other methods of Optional might be more appropriate in a different situation. For example, if you don't really care about an absent value, you can just call ifPresent() instead. And if you're only interested in reading from the Optional, you can transform it and provide a default value with .map().orElse(defaultValue).

The latter usage is quite common. Take a look at an example in the code below:

```
String state = communicator.getConnectionToEarth()
                    .map(Connection::isFree)
                    .map(isFree -> isFree ? "free" : "busy")
                    .orElse("absent");
```

What Have You Learned?

As you've seen in this chapter, the functional style really makes for a different way to program Java. You can be so much more concise if you just describe what you want to achieve instead of instructing the computer step-by-step.

If coding the imperative way still feels more natural, remember that you just might be more familiar with this style. After all, this was the way you learned first. Keep in mind that the unfamiliar is not necessarily the more complex—you just need to get used to it. But you already know the basics.

You're able to iterate over data structures more efficiently by converting them into streams, and you know how to get back into the imperative style even in complex situations. You also learned how to interleave the functional and the imperative style neatly with the help of method references when that's most appropriate—for example, to improve the testability of your methods. Anonymous classes will no longer clutter up your code with irrelevant syntax because you can just replace them with lambda expressions. You've learned how you can make your program less fragile by using Optional return types instead of null values, and how you can integrate Optionals with streams.

But it's not just about applying functional programming. You've also seen what can go wrong and where you should be extra careful. You're aware that side effects can damage the correctness of your code, and the functional style doesn't make for more readable code if there's a lot of exception handling involved. And although Optional values are helpful, you know that they're no good if you overuse them.

Believe it or not, this is the end of the core part of this book. We're really happy that you've stuck with us this far. By now, you've certainly increased your knowledge about clean and readable Java code.

Of course, when you go into professional software development, there are many more aspects to consider. So far, we've hardly touched on concurrency, and there are important things you should know about how you get from just code to a shippable product, like continuous integration and delivery. We could continue with comparisons about those topics. But if we did, the book would be 500 pages long and no one would want to read it. Instead, we'll give you a short outlook on several important aspects that we couldn't cover adequately here. In addition to a concise summary of those concepts, the last chapter will provide you with references and links to reading material that will take you into more depth for these topics. Then you'll know exactly how to continue after you've finished this book. Never stop learning!

The first 90% of the code accounts for the first 90% of the develop-
ment time. The remaining 10% of the code accounts for the other
90% of the development time.

 ➤ *Tom Cargill*

CHAPTER 9

Prepare for the Real World

You've already learned a lot about writing clean and maintainable Java code, but there's more to professional software development. Production software has a million reasons to break. And as long as it's in use, somebody will have to maintain it. User expectations grow and their perception of what they want to do with your software usually changes during usage. After some time in production, *everything* might have to be changed:

- Your software should accommodate plenty of new features, even when there's a large backlog of bugs.

- There are no longer hundreds of users, but millions using it *every* day.

- Your software no longer runs on one machine in a local data center, but on rack-sized servers in several data centers around the world.

The key to coping with this pace is to *embrace change*—that's a part of the agile philosophy. Don't view changing requirements and circumstances as annoying, but as a sign that your software is useful, and be ready to adapt on the fly. That's why you must make sure that adapting the code won't break it in unforeseeable ways. Making the code readable and maintainable, part of what this book is about, is a prerequisite for that.

In the last chapter, we'll touch on general aspects regarding building and running your software, like applying static analysis tools, automating your build so you can do continuous integration and delivery, monitoring your software in production, and speeding it up with concurrency. These things, as well as the whole chapter, are meant as an outlook and not all of them can be nicely explained in two-page code comparisons. That's why we'll deviate from the code-snippet style of the book for the final chapter. But we'll still mix a few comparisons with good (and deliberately short) textual outlines for certain techniques so you know what they're about and where you can turn for learning more.

Use Static Code Analysis Tools

In the Olympic discipline of the high jump, the athlete has to jump over a bar, and during a competition, the bar is raised higher and higher until only a single athlete can jump over it. The world record is 2.45 m. Static analysis tools provide such a bar for the quality of your code. They investigate your code and look for potential bugs or code smells. That's more than just compiling and running the tests; hence it's a higher bar you have to jump over. It's also one step closer to a realistic development and production environment. These tools are usually efficient and quick to use. Even if they're not perfect and might report false positives, they can help you catch mistakes that don't break your code but that reduce its quality.

Most of the comparisons in this book describe accidental mistakes and code smells that are in some sense similar to what static analysis tools are looking for. If you're a beginner, it can take some time for them to sink in, and you'll need practice to *spot* them in real projects. That's also the case when there's not enough time to take a step back and think about code quality—for example, when moving fast in large code bases. Of course, experienced developers will find such problems during code review, but their time is costly. Also, if you're drowning in a sea of smaller problems that a static analysis tool could have found, chances are you'll overlook the big issues that it doesn't find.

Static code analysis tools can automatically detect certain types of problems in your code beyond compile and functional errors, and some even help you to fix them. Large code bases are no problem to analyze. And the best part: many of them are open source and free to use. No one's saying you should apply every tool out there, but there's also a good reason to use at least one of them—it can also improve the quality of your code. The point of this section is to give you an overview of the most important tools for Java.

SpotBugs,[1] or its predecessor FindBugs, is one of the oldest static code analysis tools for Java. It detects over 400 types of potential bugs.[2] Yep, that's a lot. SpotBugs provides textual help only—it points you to a problematic piece of code in a report file or your IDE, but it doesn't suggest a copy and paste–ready fix. Some of the bugs it spots might be false positives, so every time you get a warning, you should check whether it's a real problem.

---

1.   https://spotbugs.github.io/
2.   https://spotbugs.readthedocs.io/en/latest/bugDescriptions.html

SpotBugs is helpful because a large community of developers worked to build good bug detection strategies.

Checkstyle[3] and PMD[4] are two other popular tools that are quite similar to SpotBugs. Their main difference is that they're highly configurable, which makes them a powerful help if you want to ensure a certain code style. The downside is they're quite verbose, and you'll usually want to configure them specifically for your project, which can be tricky. In their default configuration with a full rule set, they'll report issues in numbers that are an order of magnitude higher than for SpotBugs—some of which might even be opinionated or contradict each other. That's why we usually build a custom configuration with the rules that are important for our project, especially the ones that enforce the Java code conventions and check for the problems that are covered in this book.

Error Prone[5] is yet another popular static analysis tool that's more of an enhancement to the Java compiler. It performs more advanced type checks and, thankfully, provides suggestions for fixes to the numerous issues it can find. It's built by Google for their own Java code base, but the tool is open source. Error Prone became famous when it detected a bug[6] in ConcurrentHashMap, an API class that was in production for some time and widely believed to be bug-free. We like to use Error Prone in our projects because it produces a very low number of false positives, and if it finds something, it also provides a suggestion for a fix.

Lastly, some Java IDEs come with built-in support for static analysis. For example, the IntelliJ IDEA has a feature named Code Inspection[7] that can automatically detect issues in your code, very much like the tools we discussed above. The best part is that it also proposes fixes, and you can refactor the code with a click. Even if you're not using IntelliJ, you should check what your IDE can do for you out-of-the-box.

To sum up, static analysis tools are very useful and efficient for finding problems in your code that the compiler or tests won't find. There are plenty of tools available in the Java ecosystem, and you should apply at least one of them to help you maintain a high quality. They also help to enforce a common Java code format in your team.

3. http://checkstyle.sourceforge.net/
4. https://pmd.github.io/
5. http://errorprone.info
6. https://bugs.openjdk.java.net/browse/JDK-8176402
7. https://www.jetbrains.com/help/idea/code-inspection.html

Agree On the Java Format in Your Team

When you're building software professionally, you're doing it in a team. Admittedly, some programmers work as independent freelancers, but the vast majority work in teams. That's good, because programming in teams is more fun and you have a chance to learn from your colleagues.

Of course, there are also many challenges: you need to coordinate, plan, and communicate with each other, and agile processes such as Scrum or XP tell you how to do this. This book isn't about teamwork—it's about code quality, and we won't go any further in this direction.[8] We're bringing this up because there's a team challenge that has an impact on your code: formatting.

Code formatting is a topic that easily leads to heated debates, even when you talk about the same language. Already the length of a line of code can be discussed. Should a line of code be set to 80 characters as it has been traditionally or 120 characters because we have widescreen displays today? Maybe 100 characters is a good compromise? Probably the most famous discussion point is whether you should indent code with tabs or spaces. Few things are more controversial among developers. Ultimately, there's no right or wrong here. The problem is that all team members need to agree on a consistent formatting style to avoid constant reformatting and even bugs.

Usually, as long as you find a format everybody can agree upon, it's fine—at least as long as you don't waste countless hours trying to reach an agreement and creating corresponding configurations in your IDEs.

A better way is to avoid all discussion and use an industry standard. The Java code conventions that we've mentioned a few times are a good start, but they're comparably brief and they haven't been updated in a while. That's why we recommend you resort to the Google Java Style Guide,[9] the Java formatting guidelines by Google. Essentially, they're an updated version of the Java Code Conventions with more sensible defaults. If that works for formatting all Java Code at Google, chances are it'll also work for your team. The kicker is that there's Google Java Format,[10] a tool that checks and enforces this formatting. It's best if you make that a part of your build process. Every time you make a change, simply run the tool and you're done.

---

8. If you're interested in learning more, we recommend *Agile Software Development, Principles, Patterns, and Practices [Mar02]* by Robert C. Martin.
9. https://google.github.io/styleguide/javaguide.html
10. https://github.com/google/google-java-format

Automate Your Build

Some say that before you can run (write Java code in an IDE) you need to learn to walk (use the Java command-line tools). We think this is true for the complete build process of your software.

You might've written your first Java program in a simple text editor and used the command-line tool javac to compile your code and run it with the java command. This works as long things stay (very) simple. From our teaching experience, it also really helps beginners to get a grasp of the difference between source code and byte code.

But in any halfway realistic project, you'll be using external libraries in the form of JARs (Java Archives), executing JUnit tests, and building JavaDoc-based documentation. If you want to do this only on the command line, you'll end up with a lot of different and very long calls.

That's why almost every Java developer writes Java with an IDE such as IntelliJ IDEA, Eclipse, or NetBeans. IDEs can handle all the necessary tasks we need to perform, such as executing a Java class with a main method or debugging a single JUnit test. It's nice if you can standardize that across the team, but usually people want to work on different operating systems and/or IDEs. In that case, you can't really rely on a single IDE anymore.

The way to go is to automate your build using a dedicated build tool or language that works in the same way on all systems and independent of a developer's machine. Gradle[11] is such a tool. It's the rising star for Java and the default build system for Android, but you'll also use Apache Maven,[12] the established enterprise standard, or Apache Ant[13] often.

To automate your build, you'll need to write a build file and put it into your project. This file uses a special syntax depending on the build tool, and in it, you describe where your source code is located, what your dependencies and external libraries are, and what else you need to do for a successful build. Then, the build tool interprets the files, downloads any external libraries, runs all tests, and if successful, builds an executable. Modern IDEs can interpret those build files as well, and they integrate with the build tools so you can run anything from within your IDE. When you've automated all that, you've taken the first steps toward a true delivery pipeline.

---

11. https://gradle.org/
12. https://maven.apache.org/
13. http://ant.apache.org/

Use Continuous Integration

Automating your build locally with a build tool is really a good start. You can run your tests and build executables whenever you want locally on your developer machine. But in a real development environment, you'll want more. That's where *Continuous Integration [DMG07]* comes in.

When you make a code change locally, of course you should run unit tests to make sure you didn't break anything before you commit it to version control. But in an enterprise project, the complete set of tests can be huge, and building a fully integrated executable can take a long time. We're talking about several minutes here, even hours, and that's not a process you want to trigger for every small code change on your machine.

On top of that, we've told you to *Use Static Code Analysis Tools*, on page 150. Those tools all operate on a code base and show you potential issues in it. You might fix some issues directly and just ignore false positives. What you're most interested in is how your last changes affect code quality. Did you introduce new issues that weren't there before?

All of these things—extensive testing, integration, and code quality checks—can be outsourced to dedicated machines: continuous integration servers. The idea behind it all is very simple: for every commit to the version control system, a dedicated server pulls all code, executes all tests, and builds a fully integrated executable. It runs code quality checks and compares the results to the data from the commits before, thereby building a timeline for the quality of your code. That way, it's easy to make sure that your project is always buildable and quality doesn't go down.

There are many different tools you can use here. On your own server, you can install Jenkins,[14] one of the most popular continuous integration systems in the Java world. It can run your tests, and there are many plugins for quality checks. But you can also use a dedicated quality analysis server. Here, the market leader is SonarQube,[15] which you can host yourself or use their cloud solution. That last point is interesting. Many cloud services that you can use for testing and quality analysis, such as Travis CI[16] or Codacy,[17] are available. They're handy if your code is open source.

But just building and testing your software isn't all. You also have to deliver.

---

14. https://jenkins.io/
15. https://www.sonarqube.org/
16. https://travis-ci.org/
17. https://www.codacy.com/

Prepare for and Deliver Into Production

Production changes everything. Your customers will use your software in so many untested ways that you'll get lots of slow requests, errors, and unexpected behavior in your software. To fix those, you need insights about what causes all these problems. So it's vital to prepare for that.

One part of that preparation is to implement monitoring in the form of logs, metrics, dashboards, and alerts. First, you should *Favor Logging Over Console Output*, on page 156, which we'll explain to you in a moment. Next, you should set up a central place where all your logs go. If the logs are also searchable and you can analyze them, compute metrics, and visualize them in a dashboard, that's perfect. Then, you might be able to derive key insights and thresholds, like how many orders were placed within the last 24 hours. And if such a metric is below a target threshold, you'll probably want to alert the person who can bring that metric up again. For things like this, we can recommend the Open Source Elastic Stack[18] and Graylog.[19]

Errors and exceptions in production deserve our special attention. They're neon signs for bugs in the code and holes in the tests, which makes their stack traces and context information really valuable. That's why it's important to collect and track any exceptions that have occurred automatically. And don't forget the front end if you're building desktop, mobile, or single-page applications—a lot of exceptions happen there. We recommend Airbrake[20] for the back end and Sentry[21] for the front end.

But even if you're prepared for production, there's another issue: *How long does it take you to put a change of a single line of code into production?* Can you answer that question for your current project? The longer the time to production is, the harder it is to fix something quickly, roll back a change, or ship a new feature that's ready. Continuous integration systems are your friend here. Most of them can be configured to not only build a fully integrated system, but also to deploy it into a production environment.

Of course, we can't cover a full release strategy in this section, but if you want to know more, there's an excellent book dedicated to the topic: *Release It!* [Nyg18].

---

18. https://www.elastic.co/products
19. https://www.graylog.org/
20. https://airbrake.io/
21. https://sentry.io

Favor Logging Over Console Output

```
class LaunchChecklist {

    List<String> checks = Arrays.asList("Cabin Pressure",
                                         "Communication",
                                         "Engine");

    Status prepareAscend(Commander commander) {
        System.out.println("Prepare ascend");
        for (String check : checks) {
            if (commander.isFailing(check)) {
                System.out.println(check + " ... FAILURE");
                System.err.println("Abort take off");
                return Status.ABORT_TAKE_OFF;
            }
            System.out.println(check + " ... OK");
        }
        System.out.println("Read for take off");
        return Status.READY_FOR_TAKE_OFF;
    }
}
```

When you're lucky, you can find errors in your code just by looking at it. But oftentimes, this isn't enough and you have to run the code and investigate the memory to spot a bug. Within the development environment, you'll usually have a debugging mode you can use to halt the execution and look at the memory. But this doesn't work anymore when you've delivered the program to the production environment. In that case, you need meaningful output.

In the code above, we get an insight into the state of the program through calls to System.out.println() and System.err.println(). Errors go to System.err and all other information to System.out. With that separation, the code already provides all information we could possibly need, doesn't it?

Well, certainly not. We actually miss out on a lot. We don't know:

- at what time a statement is printed
- the number of the line of code that does the printing
- the value of the method parameter
- if all printed statements are equally important

And there's more. All statements go to the console, so we can't write a subset of the statements to a file and send the important ones via email to the people who need to know. Last but not least, string concatenation is expensive, and we do it all the time in the code above, even if we are not really interested in them.

The solution to this problem is to use a proper logging framework:

```java
class LaunchChecklist {
    private static final Logger LOGGER =
            LogManager.getLogger(LaunchChecklist.class);

    List<String> checks = Arrays.asList("Cabin Pressure",
                                        "Communication",
                                        "Engine");

    Status prepareAscend(Commander commander) {
        LOGGER.info("{}: Prepare ascend", commander);
        LOGGER.debug("{} Checks: {}", checks.size(), checks);
        for (String check : checks) {
            if (commander.isFailing(check)) {
                LOGGER.warn("{}: {} ... FAILURE", commander, check);
                LOGGER.error("{}: Abort take off!", commander);
                return Status.ABORT_TAKE_OFF;
            }
            LOGGER.info("{}: {} ... OK", commander, check);
        }
        LOGGER.info("{}: Read for take off!", commander);
        return Status.READY_FOR_TAKE_OFF;
    }
}
```

There are many logging frameworks for Java and a lot of opinionated discussion about them. From what we know, Log4j[22] is one of the most widely used, and that's why we use it here. With Log4j, you can use an internal Logger that writes class-specific messages based on a program-wide configuration.

A logger automatically writes a lot more information, which makes it easier to trace down bugs. It will log the time when it executes a statement and also the line of code. It's also fairly easy to write all context information through parameters for the statement.

We can configure the logging framework so that some log statements are stored in files, some are sent over the network, and some are even printed to the console. What's more, we can use log levels to mark the severity of a message—for example, debug, info, warn, error, or fatal—by calling the right method. At runtime, we can configure the logger to log only important messages and skip the rest. Not writing out all debug messages can make for a huge performance improvement. To sum up, there's no real downside to using a logging framework apart from adding another library to the build. That's why you're guaranteed to use them in any productive application.

---

22. Available at logging.apache.org/log4j. Supports the popular logging facade SLF4J slf4j.org.

Minimize and Isolate Multithreaded Code

So far in this chapter, we've given you hints on how to streamline your development toward a production environment. But of course, you'll also have to make sure that your program performs in production. The key to that is concurrency, leveraging the multicore capabilities of today's machines. That's something we've hardly touched upon so far, essentially because it would double the size of the book. Nevertheless, we'll give you a few basic hints and pointers to further sources in the following pages.

Concurrency isn't easy to grasp, and it's even harder to code correctly. Bugs in concurrent software can result in huge problems and even loss of life, according to *An Investigation of the Therac-25 Accidents [LT93]*. And the bad news continue: tests and static analysis are notoriously bad at ensuring the correctness of concurrent code. Although costly, manual code reviews are usually a better choice.

So what can you do in this situation? Well, first of all, avoid premature optimization and multithreaded code until you have a good reason for it, like terrible results from a performance benchmark. Your first guess should be that a sequential solution is fast enough. Only after you measure your code and it's too slow should you go for multithreading.

But if you write concurrent code, you should take care to structure your program well. We recommend that you keep multithreaded code as isolated as possible—limited to few packages in your code base, for example—and to document it thoroughly.

On top of that, you should *Favor Immutable Over Mutable State*, on page 120 as far as this is possible. Mutable data is prone to concurrency bugs, such as race conditions or lost updates. The less mutable data you use, the smaller the chance for these bugs.

That's why you should document concurrent access to mutable data in your code, especially how this data is protected from concurrency bugs. We recommend that you use the JCIP Annotations[23] stemming from the famous book *Java Concurrency in Practice [Goe06]*, which also explains all the nitty-gritty details of concurrency in Java.

---

23. http://jcip.net/annotations/doc/

Use High-Level Concurrency Abstractions

Sometimes (most of the time, actually), you just need to make your program multithreaded. For example, you might have to handle multiple users at the same time in a web application. Or maybe you've got a desktop or Android application that interacts with the user and the screen in a UI thread and executes compute-intense tasks in background threads.

In those cases, you'll typically let your threads communicate via shared memory: one thread writes a variable that another one reads, and vice versa. Java has supported such a built-in threading model and synchronization primitives since its inception. That's been one of its major advantages in comparison to other high-level languages at the time.

These primitives are keywords like volatile and synchronized, which you can use to mark critical sections in your code. You can also work with threads through the start() and join() methods of the Thread class and use wait() and notify() on any Object to let threads sleep and wake up. These primitives work, and you can build correct multithreaded programs using only them. But they're also easy to misuse, and they're tricky if you have special multithreaded requirements, such as fairness.

Concurrency primitives in Java belong to the past. The language has evolved a lot and has undergone many improvements in terms of higher-level classes for writing concurrent code. We recommend that you rely exclusively on these higher-level classes. There's more of them than we can reasonably cover here, but examples are synchronization classes such as Semaphore, CountDownLatch, or CyclingBarrier and data structures such as AtomicInteger, LongAdder, ConcurrentHashMap, CopyOnWriteArrayList, or BlockingQueue.

To use those classes correctly, you need to have a solid understanding of how the Java Memory Model and the happens-before relations between state changes in that model work. Maybe we'll write a second book about all of this one day, but if we don't get around to it, there are several excellent books on the subject out there waiting for you: *Java Concurrency in Practice [Goe06]*, which we've mentioned before, and also *Programming Concurrency on the JVM [Sub11]*.

Speed Up Your Program

```
class Inventory {

    List<Supply> supplies;

    long countDifferentKinds() {
        return supplies.stream()
                        .sequential() // this can be omitted
                        .filter(Supply::isUncontaminated)
                        .map(Supply::getName)
                        .distinct()
                        .count();
    }
}
```

Although we're not focused on concurrency in this book, we don't want to leave you without giving you one concrete hint—one comparison—that shows how you can speed up your code using concurrency. You probably recognize the code above from *Favor Functional Over Imperative Style*, on page 132.

If you look closely, you can see the call to the method sequential() in the code. This call makes sure that the whole stream processes the elements sequentially. It operates on a single element at a time. Actually, that's the default for streams created with stream()—you don't have to call the method explicitly, and we've done it here just to make the point. If the elements in the list are processed sequentially, then obviously the code will take longer to process a list with millions of supplies than a list with hundreds of them. Let's assume we've done a benchmark and found that this code is too slow for our application scenario. But what can we do *to make it faster*?

If we do the whole computation sequentially, then at most, one core of the CPU computes the result. However, today's computers (including mobile phones) have several cores, usually around 4–8. That means we can speed up the program by using all cores concurrently.

When you have a sequential stream without side effects like in the code above, there's potential to run the work in parallel by distributing the work onto several cores. We can apply the filter() operations for millions of supplies *concurrently*, because the operation depends on a supply only. As soon as an item has passed the filter, it can be immediately transformed using map(), again because this operation doesn't depend on other items. Even the distinct() and count() operators can be parallelized to some degree, although not in such a straightforward manner as the filter() and map() operators.

So how can we distribute the work onto several cores and speed up the program?

```java
class Inventory {

    List<Supply> supplies;

    long countDifferentKinds() {
        return supplies.stream()
                       .parallel()
                       .filter(Supply::isUncontaminated)
                       .map(Supply::getName)
                       .distinct()
                       .count();
    }
}
```

Normally, it takes a highly paid expert to convert sequential to parallel code. But one of the many advantages of streams is that they make parallelization a lot easier. We don't even need to write any explicitly multithreaded code.

Remember, streams define *what* should be computed, instead of listing every detail *how* the computation happens. Now we bring this paradigm to its pinnacle by just telling the stream that it should execute in parallel—without actually describing how it should do that. That's as easy as switching our stream from sequential() to parallel().

Voilà! This will parallelize the complete computation under the hood. Alternatively, you can directly create a parallel stream from any Collection with stream-Parallel(). But a lot of other methods don't provide such a convenient method when creating a parallel stream, so parallel() is the more versatile one.

Sometimes it's as easy as this to get an n-times better performance, where n is equal to the number of cores available on the system. Internally, the JVM provides a thread pool that's shared for all parallel streams.

But be aware that this solution works only when you have a stream without side effects and where single processing steps are independent. There's a considerable overhead if you use operations that force the stream to synchronize again, such as sort() or forEachOrdered(). In that case, the sequential() option might actually be faster. So, when you try to improve performance in this way, you should always benchmark your code and make sure that your improvements have the intended effect.

Note that you can't parallelize parts of a stream. If you include multiple calls to sequential() or parallel() in the stream, then the last call wins.

Know Your Falsehoods

```
class NameTag {

    final String name;

    NameTag(String fullName) {
        this.name = parse(fullName).toUpperCase();
    }

    String parse(String fullName) {
        String[] components = fullName.split("[,| ]");
        if (components == null || components.length < 2) {
            return fullName;
        }
        if (fullName.contains(",")) {
            return components[0];
        } else {
            return components[components.length - 1];
        }
    }
}
```

We'd like to end the book with a peculiar comparison. No matter what domain you're in, your code's just as good as your understanding of the real world and no better. And the real world is complex. That's why you shouldn't assume too much and make your code flexible to cope with being proven wrong.

The code above shows a NameTag class that takes the full name of a person and transforms it into a specific format for name tags. For example, "Neil Alden Armstrong" gets the name tag "ARMSTRONG." We're assuming that full names are provided in a regular format, separated by either a whitespace or a comma. That's either with first and second names before the last name, or the inverse, the last name before the first separated with a comma.

A lot of the assumptions in this format will break easily. The name of the second man on the moon is "Edwin Eugene Aldrin, Jr." Here, our algorithm returns "EDWIN," which is his first name. Names are complicated, and there are many more things that can go wrong. Take a look at this table:

Name	Computed Tag	Expected Tag	Correct?
Neil Alden Armstrong	ARMSTRONG	ARMSTRONG	✓
Edwin Eugene Aldrin, Jr.	EDWIN	ALDRIN	✗
費俊龍	費俊龍	費	✗

So what should we do when our assumptions are proven to be false?

```java
class NameTag {

    final String name;

    NameTag(String name) {
        Objects.requireNonNull(name);
        this.name = name;
    }
}
```

Starting out with the table, we *can* build unit tests and code a solution for those names. But this is just a small sample of a few ways to spell out or format names, and it might well be incomplete. In a realistic setting, you'll have many more combinations and many that haven't been spelled out.

There's a simpler and better solution to all of this. You shouldn't assume too much in your code and just pass that task to the user of the class. Let her set the name tag directly and accept any valid non-null String as a tag name. After all, if you don't know too much about a format, it's best to assume as little as possible.

That might seem strange. But have a look at the overview of personal names around the world by the W3C.[24] Names can be complicated indeed. Every culture has its own ways (yes, multiple ones!) of writing names. Without any context, it's impossible to determine which part of a name is the last name.

Some names, even simple ones, are special in other ways, and that can cause problems. Look at the case of Christopher Null[25] whose last name is, well, "Null"—something that prevents him from submitting a lot of forms in the web. Some frameworks and programs interpret his name as a null reference—and prevent this poor guy from entering his name into forms.

But the list of falsehoods[26] doesn't stop here. Email addresses, postal codes, CSV files, and our favorite: time zones. It's an incredibly challenging task to *correctly* calculate the difference in minutes between two localized daytimes.

The point is to make you aware that you should be careful with assumptions when you program. In theory, they may seem fine. But they often break in practice. Always think twice before you let your code be guided by sheer assumptions to make your code ready for the real world!

---

24. https://www.w3.org/International/questions/qa-personal-names.en
25. https://www.wired.com/2015/11/null/
26. https://github.com/kdeldycke/awesome-falsehood

What Have You Learned?

You've made it! This is the end of this book. We're happy that you've taken this journey with us, and we hope you'll remember: the journey's the reward. You've learned so much along the way.

We covered 70 examples, including code style, comments, naming, exceptions, testing, object-oriented design, and functional programming to sharpen your understanding of high-quality code.

Now, you're able to

- Spot problematic Java code quickly and know how to improve it.
- Recognize common types of bugs and know how to avoid them.
- Explain why one code is clean and another isn't.

And not just that... In this last chapter, you learned the basic idea for a lot of best practices in real software development. It's about going all the way to production from static code analysis, an agreed upon code format, an automated build, and integration to the final delivery. You're aware of concurrency as the tool that will make your program perform in the real world, but also that you have to be careful when applying it. After all, great power comes with great risks and, in this case, new types of bugs. And last, you learned that you always have to challenge your assumptions about the world when you program.

We've referenced many good books throughout the comparisons, so if you're hungry for more, you know where to continue. If you haven't read them yet, there are two classics we want to recommend over and over again:

- *Effective Java [Blo18]*
- *Clean Code [Mar08]*

Our book's subtitle promised to help you "Become a Java Craftsman in 70 Examples." Obviously, it's not just about reading the book, but about applying the principles in practice. So be sure to practice. And when you do, use the comparisons in this book to help you to produce better code. Watch out for problems, and apply solutions in the code you write and in the code you review, because becoming a Java Craftsman is also (read: all) about experience!

Bibliography

[Blo18]   Joshua Bloch. *Effective Java*. Addison-Wesley, Boston, MA, 2018.

[DMG07]   Paul Duvall, Steve Matyas, and Andrew Glover. *Continuous Integration: Improving Software Quality and Reducing Risk*. Addison-Wesley, Boston, MA, 2007.

[DMHL18]   Linus Dietz, Johannes Manner, Simon Harrer, and Jörg Lenhard. Teaching Clean Code. *Proceedings of the 1st Workshop on Innovative Software Engineering Education*. 2018, March.

[GHJV95]   Erich Gamma, Richard Helm, Ralph Johnson, and John Vlissides. *Design Patterns: Elements of Reusable Object-Oriented Software*. Addison-Wesley, Boston, MA, 1995.

[Goe06]   Brian Goetz. *Java Concurrency in Practice*. Addison-Wesley, Boston, MA, 2006.

[Gol91]   David Goldberg. What Every Computer Scientist Should Know About Floating-Point Arithmetic. *Computing Surveys*. 23[1], 1991.

[LHT15]   Jeff Langr, Andy Hunt, and Dave Thomas. *Pragmatic Unit Testing in Java 8 with JUnit*. The Pragmatic Bookshelf, Raleigh, NC, 2015.

[LT93]   Nancy Leveson and Clark Turner. An Investigation of the Therac-25 Accidents. *IEEE Computer*. 26[7], 1993.

[Mar02]   Robert C. Martin. *Agile Software Development, Principles, Patterns, and Practices*. Prentice Hall, Englewood Cliffs, NJ, 2002.

[Mar08]   Robert C. Martin. *Clean Code: A Handbook of Agile Software Craftsmanship*. Prentice Hall, Englewood Cliffs, NJ, 2008.

[Nyg18]   Michael Nygard. *Release It! Second Edition*. The Pragmatic Bookshelf, Raleigh, NC, 2018.

[Sub11]   Venkat Subramaniam. *Programming Concurrency on the JVM*. The Pragmatic Bookshelf, Raleigh, NC, 2011.

[Sub14]   Venkat Subramaniam. *Functional Programming in Java*. The Pragmatic Bookshelf, Raleigh, NC, 2014.

[ZCTZ13]   Uwe Zdun, Rafael Capilla, Huy Tran, and Olaf Zimmermann. Sustainable Architectural Design Decisions. *IEEE Software*. 30[6], 2013.

Index

SYMBOLS

% (percent sign), format strings, 33
< character
  escaping in JavaDoc comments, 55
  format strings, 33
[] (brackets), Booleans, 8
{} (braces)
  avoiding switch fallthrough, 14
  lambdas, 131
  parameterized tests, 109

A

abbreviations, avoiding, 66
abstract types, favoring over concrete types, 118
abstractions and concurrency, 159
Agile Software Development, 152
Airbrake, 155
alerts, preparing for production, 155
Android, 153
anonymous classes, favoring lambdas over, 130
Apache Ant, 153
Apache Maven, 153
Apple, 15
arguments, order in testing, 98
assertAll(), 97
assertArrayEquals(), 97

assertEquals(), 97–98
assertFalse(), 97
assertIterableEquals(), 97
assertLinesMatch(), 97
assertNotEquals(), 97
assertSame(), 97
assertThrows(), 103
assertTimeout(), 97
assertTrue(), 96
assertions
  argument order, 98
  grouping multiple, 97
  using meaningful, 96
assessment, self, xvii
auto-indentation, 15
AutoCloseable, 87
automating builds, 153
averagingLong(), 139

B

Beck, Kent, 16
before/after approach, xv, xix
@BeforeAll, 106
@BeforeEach, 106
behavior, combining state and, 122
best practices, *see* design principles
BigDecimal, 101
Booleans
  avoiding NullPointerException, 10
  avoiding negations, 4
  avoiding unnecessary comparisons, 2

  brackets for, 8
  getter and setter names, 63
  grouping to simplify, 8
  returning directly, 6
  splitting methods with Boolean parameters, 114
braces ({})
  avoiding switch fallthrough, 14
  lambdas, 131
  parameterized tests, 109
brackets ([]), Booleans, 8
break statements, avoiding switch fallthrough, 12
brevity and names, 68
builds, automating, 153

C

camelCase, 61
CamelCase, 60
CAPITAL_SNAKE_CASE, 61
case, Java naming conventions, 60
cast, type checking before, 84
catching
  explaining empty catch, 90
  most specific exception, 76
  multi-catch block, 77
cause chain
  avoiding breaking, 80
  breaking in tests, 102
change, need to embrace, 149
check, 25

checked exceptions and
   streams, 140
Checkstyle, xxi, 151
CI (continuous integration),
   154–155
ClassCastException, 84
classes
   favoring lambdas over
      anonymous classes,
      130
   JavaDoc comments, 52
   method references and
      names, 135
   names, 69, 135
   synchronization classes,
      159
   utility classes, 35
ClassNotFoundException, 85
Clean Code, xvi, 31, 164
clean code, developing sense
   of, xvi, xviii
close(), 86
closing
   resources always, 86–89
   resources, multiple, 88
   streams, 140–141
Codacy, 154
code
   for this book, xx, xxii
   code symmetry, 16
   format conventions for
      team, 152
   removing commented-out
      code, 40
   restoring removed, 41
Code Inspection in IntelliJ
   IDEA, 151
code quality
   code symmetry, 16
   defined, xi
   developing sense of, xvi,
      xviii
   teaching approach, xvii
code symmetry, 16
codewars.com, xviii
collect(), 137–138
collections
   avoiding modification
      during iteration, 26
   avoiding side effects, 136
   favoring functional style
      over imperative, 132
   terminating complex
      streams, 138
   turning streams into, 135

comments, 37–58
   documenting design deci-
      sions, 39, 46, 48
   enabling in regular ex-
      pressions, 48
   ignored exceptions, 91
   importance of, 37, 58
   JavaDoc, 50–57
   JavaDoc classes and in-
      terfaces, 52
   JavaDoc constructors, 56
   JavaDoc methods, 54, 56
   JavaDoc packages, 50
   removing commented-out
      code, 40
   removing superfluous, 38
   replacing with constants,
      42
   replacing with utility
      methods, 44
   templates, 47, 91
   test code, 95
   using examples in, 48, 53
COMMENTS flag, 48
comparison approach, xv, xix
comparisons, avoiding unnecessary, 2
compile(), 29
compiling, regular expressions, 29
computeIfAbsent(), 130
concrete types, favoring abstract types over, 118
concurrency
   abstractions, 159
   minimizing and isolating
      multithreaded code,
      158
   performance and, 158,
      160
   primitives, 159
ConcurrentHashMap, 151
ConcurrentModificationException, 26
CONDITION -> EFFECT template,
   91
conditionals
   avoiding NullPointerException,
      10
   avoiding negations, 4
   avoiding unnecessary
      comparisons, 2
   De Morgan's laws, 7
   grouping into separate
      methods, 7–8
   returning Booleans direct-
      ly, 6

console output, favoring logging over console, 156–157
constants
   favoring enums over inte-
      ger constants, 22
   names, 21, 43, 61
   replacing comments with,
      42
   replacing magic numbers
      with, 20, 42
constructors
   avoiding breaking cause
      chain, 81
   calling, 57
   exception messages, 81,
      83
   getter and setter names,
      63
   JavaDoc comments, 56
Continuous Integration, 154
continuous integration (CI),
   154–155
conventions
   for this book, xix
   getters and setters in
      frameworks, 62
   Java code conventions,
      61, 152
   Java naming, 60
   single vs. multiple return
      statements, 3
   style guides, 152
   for team, 152
Copernicus, Nicolaus, 129
copying, defensive, 125
count(), 133, 137, 160
curly braces, *see* braces
cyber-dojo, xviii

D

dashboards, preparing for
   production, 155
De Morgan's laws, 7
decimal precision, 100
default case, avoiding switch
   fallthrough, 13
defensive copying, 125
delivery, preparing for, 155
delta, 101
dependencies, common se-
   tups and implicit, 107
Design Patterns, 128
design principles, 113–128
   about, 113, 128

combining state and be-
havior, 122
developing sense of, 115
favoring abstract types
over concrete types,
118
favoring immutable state
over mutable state,
120, 158
leaky references, avoid-
ing, 124
null, avoiding returning,
126
splitting methods with
Boolean parameters,
114
splitting methods with
optional parameters,
116
state and, 120–123, 158
development, *see* professional
development
disabled tests, 105
@Disabled...TODO format, 105
@DisplayName, 105
distinct(), 133, 160
documentation, *see al-
so* JavaDoc
comments as, 39, 46, 48
concurrency, 158
with examples, 48, 53
Domain Name System (DNS),
60
domain-specific names, 70
double, 101
duplication
avoiding negations, 5
lambda duplication, 135
dynamic object types, checking type before cast, 84

E
edge cases, 110
Effective Java, xvi, 164
empty(), 143
enums, favoring over integer
constants, 22
error messages
explaining cause in, 78
exposing cause in, 82
Error Prone, xxi, 151
errors, 73–92
about, 73, 92
always closing multiple
resources, 88

always closing resources,
86–89
avoiding breaking cause
chain, 80
avoiding exceptions in
streams, 140
avoiding switch
fallthrough, 13
catching most specific
exception, 76
checking type before cast,
84
collecting and tracking,
155–157
exception handling by
JUnit, 102
explaining cause in mes-
sages, 78
explaining empty catch,
90
exposing cause in mes-
sages, 82
failing fast, 74
multi-catch block, 77
escaping < character in
JavaDoc comments, 55
examples
in JavaDoc comments, 53
using in comments, 48,
53
Exception type, 76
exceptions
avoiding breaking cause
chain, 80
avoiding in streams, 140
catching most specific, 76
checked, 140
checking type before cast,
84
collecting and tracking,
155–157
explaining cause in mes-
sages, 78
explaining empty catch,
90
exposing cause in mes-
sages, 82
handling by JUnit, 102
ignoring, 91
multi-catch block, 77
throwing to avoid return-
ing null, 127

F
factory methods, 56
fail fast, 74
fail(), 102

false positives in static code
analysis tools, 150
falsehoods, 162
feedback, resources on, xviii
fields
avoiding Optional, 144
getter and setter names,
63
names, 61
files, open options, 11
filter(), 133, 135, 147, 160
filtering(), 139
filters, lambdas, 133, 135,
147, 160
final keyword
avoiding leaky references,
124
favoring immutable over
mutable state, 121
replacing magic numbers
with constants, 21
FindBugs, xxi, 150
Fizz Buzz Test, xvii
FizzBuzz Test, self-assessment with, xvii
flatMap(), 141, 147
flatMapping(), 139
float, 100
floating-point numbers, 100
for loops, favoring for-each over,
24
for-each loops
favoring over for loops, 24
iterator basis, 27
forEach(), avoiding side effects,
136
format strings vs. string concatenation, 32
format(), 33
frameworks
combining state and be-
havior, 123
getters and setters name
conventions, 62
logging, 156–157
frequency(), 35
functional programming,
129–148
about, 129, 148
avoiding Optional fields or
parameters, 144
avoiding exceptions in
streams, 140
avoiding side effects, 136

favoring Optional over null, 142

favoring functional style over imperative, 132, 146

favoring lambdas over anonymous classes, 130

favoring method references over lambdas, 134

terminating complex streams, 138

using Optionals as streams, 146

Functional Programming in Java, 133

G

getConversionRate(), 42

getters
avoiding Optional fields or parameters, 144
avoiding leaky references, 125
names, 62, 145

Git, 41

given-when-then testing structure, 94, 107

Google
Error Prone, xxi, 151
Java Format, 152
Java Style Guide, 152

Google Java Format, 152

Google Java Style Guide, 152

Gradle, 153

Graylog, 155

grouping
Booleans, 8
combining state and behavior, 122
conditionals into separate, 7–8
formatting test code, 95
multiple assertions, 97
with new lines, 30, 95
streams, 139

groupingBy(), 139

H

happy path, 73

hasNext(), 27

Hibernate, 62

Hoare, Tony, 127

I

IDEs
about, 153
auto-indentation, 15
automating builds, 153
static code analysis tools, 151

IEEE Standard for Floating-Point Arithmetic (IEEE 754), 100

if statements
avoiding null in functional programming, 142
code symmetry example, 16
using braces to avoid switch fallthrough, 14

ifPresent(), 143, 147

ignoring, exceptions, 91

immutable state
concurrency and, 158
favoring over mutable state, 120, 158

imperative style, favoring functional style over, 132, 146

implicit dependencies and common setups, 107

indentation
auto-indentation, 15
readability and, 14

index, iteration, 24

IndexOutOfBoundsException, 24

integers, favoring enums over integer constants, 22

IntelliJ IDEA, 151

interfaces
favoring abstract types over concrete types, 118
JavaDoc comments, 52

An Investigation of the Therac-25 Accidents, 158

IOException, 140

iOS SSL/TLS protocol, 15

isolating, multithreaded code, 158

iteration
avoiding collection modifications, 26
for-each vs. for loops, 24
with index, 24
with iterators, 25
performance, 28

iterators, 25

J

Jackson, 62

Java, *see also* JavaDoc
code conventions, 61, 152
favoring Java API over DIY approach, 34
functional programming and Java 8, 129
Java 9, xvi
name conventions, 60
size of Java API, 35–36
version, xvi

java command, 153

Java Concurrency in Practice, 158–159

Java Format (Google), 152

Java Memory Model, 159

Java Style Guide (Google), 152

JavaBeans, 62, 145

javac, 153

JavaDoc, 50–57
about, 50
classes and interfaces comments, 52
constructors comments, 56
methods comments, 54, 56
package comments, 50
stream API guide, 133

JCIP Annotations, 158

Jenkins, 154

JGiven, 95

join(), 159

joining(), 139

JUnit, 93–112
about, 93, 112
describing tests, 104
edge cases, 110
exception handling, 102
expected before actual value, 98
favoring standalone tests, 106
given-when-then structure, 94, 107
order of arguments, 98
parameterized tests, 108
test names, 104, 109
tolerance values, 100
using meaningful assertions, 96

junit-quickcheck, 109

K

Klingon, 111

L

lambdas
  avoiding Optional fields or parameters, 144
  avoiding side effects, 136
  duplication, 135
  favoring Optional over null, 142
  favoring functional style over imperative, 132, 146
  favoring method references over, 134
  favoring over anonymous classes, 130
  one-liner vs. multi-liner, 131
  removeIf() and, 27
  testing, 134
  type declaration and inference, 131
  using Optionals as streams, 146

language support, 111

leaky references, avoiding, 124

line breaks
  format strings, 33
  formatting test code with, 95
  grouping with, 30, 95

logging, favoring over console output, 156–157

logical negation, lambdas, 134

logs
  favoring logging over console output, 156–157
  preparing for production, 155

long, 101

M

magic numbers, replacing with constants, 20, 42

MalformedMessageException, 83

map(), 133, 147, 160

mapping(), 139

Martin, Robert C., 31

matches(), performance and, 28

maxBy(), 139

memory and concurrency abstractions, 159

messages, error
  explaining cause in, 78
  exposing cause in, 82

messages, testing
  meaningful assertions in error messages, 96
  order of arguments, 98

methods
  combining state and behavior, 122
  factory methods, 56
  favoring method references over lambdas, 134
  grouping conditionals into separate, 8
  grouping conditionals into separate methods, 7
  JavaDoc comments, 54, 56
  names, 61, 69, 104, 115
  parameterized tests, 108
  replacing comments with utility methods, 44
  splitting methods with Boolean parameters, 114
  splitting methods with optional parameters, 116
  testing and names, 104
  utility methods, 44
  validation order, 10

metrics, preparing for production, 155

minimizing and isolating multithreaded code, 158

module-info.java file, 50

modules, JavaDoc, 50

money, representing in code, 101

multi-catch block, 77

multithreaded code
  concurrency abstractions, 159
  minimizing and isolating, 158

mutable state
  concurrency and, 158
  favoring mutable state over, 120, 158

N

%n, format strings, 33

names, 59–72
  avoiding abbreviations, 66

  avoiding hard to distinguish letters, 64
  avoiding meaningless terms, 68
  avoiding single-letter, 64
  brevity and, 68
  classes, 69, 135
  constants, 21, 43, 61
  domain-specific, 70
  exception variables when ignoring, 91
  fields, 61
  getters and setters, 62, 145
  importance of, 59, 72
  Java naming conventions, 60
  methods, 61, 69, 104, 115
  packages, 60, 69
  parameters, 61, 69
  of people, 162
  replacing magic numbers with constants, 21
  scope and, 70
  tests, 104, 109
  types, 69
  variables, 21, 25, 61, 64, 91

negations
  avoiding, 4
  logical, 134

new lines
  format strings, 33
  formatting test code with, 95
  grouping with, 30, 95

next(), 27

notify(), 159

null
  avoiding NullPointerException in conditionals, 10
  avoiding Optional fields or parameters, 144
  avoiding leaky references, 125
  avoiding returning, 126
  avoiding switch fallthrough, 12
  favoring Optional over, 142
  generic null object, 143
  null object pattern, 127
  passing as argument, 10
  returning Booleans directly, 6

splitting methods with
optional parameters,
117
validation order, 10
null object pattern, 127
Null, Christopher, 163
NullPointerException
avoiding in conditionals,
10
avoiding returning null,
126
favoring Optional over null,
142
returning Booleans directly, 6
splitting methods with
optional parameters,
117
NumberFormatException, 77

O
objects
favoring immutable over
mutable state, 120,
158
value objects, 121
Objects.requireNonNull(), 145
ofNullable(), 143, 145
Open Source Elastic Stack,
155
Optional
avoiding Optional fields or
parameters, 144
favoring over null, 142
using as streams, 146
optional parameters, splitting
methods with, 116
orElse(), 147
orElseGet(), 147
orElseThrow(), 147
order
arguments in assertions,
98
validation order, 10
output
favoring logging over console output, 156–157
format strings vs. string
concatenation, 32

P
package-info.java file, 50
packages
JavaDoc comments, 50
names, 60, 69

parallel(), 161
parallelization, 160
parameterized tests, 108
@ParameterizedTest, 109
parameters
avoiding Optional, 144
data types, 110
names, 61, 69
parameterized tests, 108
splitting methods with
Boolean parameters,
114
splitting methods with
optional parameters,
116
validation order, 10
validation, need for, 11
partitioningBy(), 139
Pattern class, 28
percent sign (%), format
strings, 33
performance
concurrency and, 158,
160
iteration, 28
parallelization, 160
regular expressions, 28
vs. understandability,
128
Play Framework, 62
PMD, xxi, 151
postconditions, constructors,
57
Pragmatic Unit Testing in Java
8 with JUnit, 112
precision, decimal precision,
100
preconditions, constructors,
57
printf(), format strings, 33
private, getter and setter
names, 63
production
concurrency abstrac-
tions, 159
falsehoods, 162
favoring logging over console output, 156–157
minimizing and isolating
multithreaded code,
158
parallelization, 160
preparing for, 155
time to, 155

professional development
change and, 149
game comparison, 19
practice and, xviii, 164
Programming Concurrency on
the JVM, 159
Project Euler, xviii
public, getter and setter names,
63

R
readability, 1–18
assertion messages, 98
avoiding NullPointerException
in conditionals, 10
avoiding abbreviations,
66
avoiding meaningless
terms, 68
avoiding negations, 4
avoiding single-letter
names, 64
avoiding switch
fallthrough, 12, 14, 16
avoiding unnecessary
comparisons, 2
braces and, 14
brevity and, 68
code quality and, xi
code symmetry, 16
condensing code with Ja-
va API, 35
domain-specific names,
70
favoring enums over inte-
ger constants, 22
favoring functional style
over imperative, 132,
146
favoring lambdas over
anonymous classes,
130
favoring method refer-
ences over lambdas,
134
favoring standalone tests,
106
for-each vs. for loops, 24
format strings vs. string
concatenation, 32
grouping with new lines,
30
importance of, 1, 18
indentation, 14
output, 32
removing commented-out
code, 40

removing superfluous comments, 38
replacing comments with constants, 42
replacing comments with utility methods, 44
replacing magic numbers with constants, 20, 42
returning Booleans directly, 6
simplifying Booleans by grouping, 8
splitting methods with Boolean parameters, 114
splitting methods with optional parameters, 116
test code, 94, 98, 106
reduce(), 137
reducing(), 139
references
    avoiding leaky, 124
    favoring method references over lambdas, 134
regular expressions
    COMMENTS flag, 48
    compiling, 29
    execution, 29
    performance, 28
    using examples in comments, 48
Release It!, 155
remove(), 27
removeIf(), 27
requireNonNull(), 12, 35
reset(), 145
resource leaks, 86
resources
    always closing, 86–89
    always closing multiple, 88
    closing streams, 140–141
resources for this book
    book pages and forum, xxii
    code files, xx, xxii
    coding skills, xviii
    concurrency, 158
    design, 128
    streams, 133
return statements, single vs. multiple, 3

S

self-assessment, xvii
Sentry, 155
separation of concerns
    code symmetry, 17
    switch fallthrough and, 13
sequential(), 160
setters
    avoiding Optional fields or parameters, 144
    avoiding leaky references, 125
    names, 62, 145
setup methods, test readability and, 106
shared memory, concurrency abstractions, 159
side effects, avoiding, 136
single-letter names, avoiding, 64
SonarQube, 154
spaces in test descriptions, 105
splitting
    methods with Boolean parameters, 114
    methods with optional parameters, 116
SpotBugs, xxi, 150
Spring, 69
square brackets, see brackets
SSL/TLS protocol, 15
StandardOpenOption, 11
start(), 159
state
    combining behavior and, 122
    concurrency and, 158
    favoring immutable state over mutable state, 120, 158
static code analysis tools, xxi, 150–151, 158
static modifier, 21
stream(), 133
streamParallel(), 161
streams
    avoiding exceptions in, 140
    avoiding side effects, 136
    checking type before cast, 84
    closing, 140–141
    favoring functional style over imperative, 132, 146
    grouping, 139
    parallelization, 160
    resources on, 133
    terminating complex, 138
    turning into collections, 135
    using Optional as, 146
strings, format strings vs. string concatenation, 32
StringTemplate, 33
summingInt(), 139
Sustainable Architectural Design Decisions, 47
switch fallthrough, avoiding, 12, 14, 16
symbols in test descriptions, 105
symmetry, code, 16
synchronization classes, 159

T

Teaching Clean Code, xvii
teaching code skills, see also professional development approach, xvii
    resources on, xviii
templates
    comments, 47, 91
    exception messages, 79, 83
    ignored exceptions, 91
test-driven development, 112
testing, 93–112
    comments, test code, 95
    concurrency and, 158
    describing tests, 104
    disabled tests, noting, 105
    edge cases, 110
    exception handling by JUnit, 102
    expected before actual value, 98
    favoring standalone tests, 106
    given-when-then structure, 94, 107
    importance of, 93, 112
    lambdas, 134
    order of arguments, 98
    parameterized tests, 108
    readability, 94, 98, 106

self-assessment with FizzBuzz Test, xvii
test cases from exception messages, 79
test names, 104, 109
test-driven development, 112
tolerance values, 100
using meaningful assertions, 96
then in given-when-then testing structure, 94, 107
thresholds, preparing for production, 155
Throwable
    about, 76
    avoiding breaking cause chain, 81
throwing
    avoiding breaking cause chain, 80
    avoiding switch fallthrough, 13
    explaining exceptions cause in messages, 78
    exposing exceptions cause in messages, 82
    with JUnit, 103
    to avoid returning null, 127
time to production, 155
TimeUnit, 35
TODO in comments, 39
tolerance values, 100
training, see professional development; teaching code skills

Travis CI, 154
try-with-resources construct
    closing resources, 87–88
    closing streams, 141
type checking
    before cast, 84
    static code analysis tools, 151
type inference, lambdas, 131
type system, see also type checking
    favoring abstract types over concrete types, 118
    favoring enums over integer constants, 22
    lambdas, 131
    type declaration and inference, 131
    type names, 69

U
UncheckedIOException, 140
unit testing, see JUnit; testing
Using FizzBuzz to Find Developers who Grok Coding, xvii
utility classes, 35
utility methods, 44

V
validation
    failing fast, 74
    order, 10
    parameters, when to use, 11

value objects and immutability, 121
values
    expected before actual, 98
    representing money in code, 101
    tolerance values, 100
@ValueSource, 109
variables
    for-each loops, 25
    names, 21, 25, 61, 64, 91
    replacing magic numbers with constants, 21
version control systems, 41
vertical space
    formatting test code, 95
    grouping with new lines, 31
    JavaDoc comments, 51–52

W
W3C, 163
wait(), 159
walk(), 140
What Every Computer Scientist Should Know About Floating-Point Arithmetic, 100
when in given-when-then testing structure, 94, 107
while loop, 27
write(), 11

Thank you!

How did you enjoy this book? Please let us know. Take a moment and email us at support@pragprog.com with your feedback. Tell us your story and you could win free ebooks. Please use the subject line "Book Feedback."

Ready for your next great Pragmatic Bookshelf book? Come on over to https://pragprog.com and use the coupon code BUYANOTHER2018 to save 30% on your next ebook.

Void where prohibited, restricted, or otherwise unwelcome. Do not use ebooks near water. If rash persists, see a doctor. Doesn't apply to *The Pragmatic Programmer* ebook because it's older than the Pragmatic Bookshelf itself. Side effects may include increased knowledge and skill, increased marketability, and deep satisfaction. Increase dosage regularly.

And thank you for your continued support,

Andy Hunt, Publisher

SAVE 30%!
Use coupon code
BUYANOTHER2018

Fix Your Hidden Problems

From technical debt to deployment in the very real, very messy world, we've got the tools you need to fix the hidden problems before they become disasters.

Software Design X-Rays

Are you working on a codebase where cost overruns, death marches, and heroic fights with legacy code monsters are the norm? Battle these adversaries with novel ways to identify and prioritize technical debt, based on behavioral data from how developers work with code. And that's just for starters. Because good code involves social design, as well as technical design, you can find surprising dependencies between people and code to resolve coordination bottlenecks among teams. Best of all, the techniques build on behavioral data that you already have: your version-control system. Join the fight for better code!

Adam Tornhill
(274 pages) ISBN: 9781680502725. $45.95
https://pragprog.com/book/atevol

Release It! Second Edition

A single dramatic software failure can cost a company millions of dollars—but can be avoided with simple changes to design and architecture. This new edition of the best-selling industry standard shows you how to create systems that run longer, with fewer failures, and recover better when bad things happen. New coverage includes DevOps, microservices, and cloud-native architecture. Stability antipatterns have grown to include systemic problems in large-scale systems. This is a must-have pragmatic guide to engineering for production systems.

Michael Nygard
(376 pages) ISBN: 9781680502398. $47.95
https://pragprog.com/book/mnee2

Level Up

From data structures to architecture and design, we have what you need.

A Common-Sense Guide to Data Structures and Algorithms

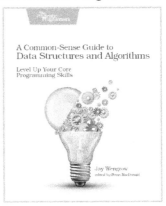

If you last saw algorithms in a university course or at a job interview, you're missing out on what they can do for your code. Learn different sorting and searching techniques, and when to use each. Find out how to use recursion effectively. Discover structures for specialized applications, such as trees and graphs. Use Big O notation to decide which algorithms are best for your production environment. Beginners will learn how to use these techniques from the start, and experienced developers will rediscover approaches they may have forgotten.

Jay Wengrow
(218 pages) ISBN: 9781680502442. $45.95
https://pragprog.com/book/jwdsal

Design It!

Don't engineer by coincidence—design it like you mean it! Grounded by fundamentals and filled with practical design methods, this is the perfect introduction to software architecture for programmers who are ready to grow their design skills. Ask the right stakeholders the right questions, explore design options, share your design decisions, and facilitate collaborative workshops that are fast, effective, and fun. Become a better programmer, leader, and designer. Use your new skills to lead your team in implementing software with the right capabilities—and develop awesome software!

Michael Keeling
(358 pages) ISBN: 9781680502091. $41.95
https://pragprog.com/book/mkdsa

Long Live the Command Line!

Use tmux and Vim for incredible mouse-free productivity.

tmux 2

Your mouse is slowing you down. The time you spend context switching between your editor and your consoles eats away at your productivity. Take control of your environment with tmux, a terminal multiplexer that you can tailor to your workflow. With this updated second edition for tmux 2.3, you'll customize, script, and leverage tmux's unique abilities to craft a productive terminal environment that lets you keep your fingers on your keyboard's home row.

Brian P. Hogan
(102 pages) ISBN: 9781680502213. $21.95
https://pragprog.com/book/bhtmux2

Modern Vim

Turn Vim into a full-blown development environment using Vim 8's new features and this sequel to the beloved bestseller *Practical Vim*. Integrate your editor with tools for building, testing, linting, indexing, and searching your codebase. Discover the future of Vim with Neovim: a fork of Vim that includes a built-in terminal emulator that will transform your workflow. Whether you choose to switch to Neovim or stick with Vim 8, you'll be a better developer.

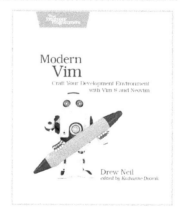

Drew Neil
(166 pages) ISBN: 9781680502626. $39.95
https://pragprog.com/book/modvim

More on Java

Get up to date on the latest Java 8 features, and take an in-depth look at concurrency options.

Functional Programming in Java

Get ready to program in a whole new way. *Functional Programming in Java* will help you quickly get on top of the new, essential Java 8 language features and the functional style that will change and improve your code. This short, targeted book will help you make the paradigm shift from the old imperative way to a less error-prone, more elegant, and concise coding style that's also a breeze to parallelize. You'll explore the syntax and semantics of lambda expressions, method and constructor references, and functional interfaces. You'll design and write applications better using the new standards in Java 8 and the JDK.

Venkat Subramaniam
(196 pages) ISBN: 9781937785468. $33
https://pragprog.com/book/vsjava8

Programming Concurrency on the JVM

Stop dreading concurrency hassles and start reaping the pure power of modern multicore hardware. Learn how to avoid shared mutable state and how to write safe, elegant, explicit synchronization-free programs in Java or other JVM languages including Clojure, JRuby, Groovy, or Scala.

Venkat Subramaniam
(280 pages) ISBN: 9781934356760. $35
https://pragprog.com/book/vspcon

Learn Why, Then Learn How

Get started on your Elixir journey today.

Adopting Elixir

Adoption is more than programming. Elixir is an exciting new language, but to successfully get your application from start to finish, you're going to need to know more than just the language. You need the case studies and strategies in this book. Learn the best practices for the whole life of your application, from design and team-building, to managing stakeholders, to deployment and monitoring. Go beyond the syntax and the tools to learn the techniques you need to develop your Elixir application from concept to production.

Ben Marx, José Valim, Bruce Tate
(242 pages) ISBN: 9781680502527. $42.95
https://pragprog.com/book/tvmelixir

Programming Elixir ≥ 1.6

This book is *the* introduction to Elixir for experienced programmers, completely updated for Elixir 1.6 and beyond. Explore functional programming without the academic overtones (tell me about monads just one more time). Create concurrent applications, but get them right without all the locking and consistency headaches. Meet Elixir, a modern, functional, concurrent language built on the rock-solid Erlang VM. Elixir's pragmatic syntax and built-in support for metaprogramming will make you productive and keep you interested for the long haul. Maybe the time is right for the Next Big Thing. Maybe it's Elixir.

Dave Thomas
(398 pages) ISBN: 9781680502992. $47.95
https://pragprog.com/book/elixir16

The Joy of Math and Healthy Programming

Rediscover the joy and fascinating weirdness of pure mathematics, and learn how to take a healthier approach to programming.

Good Math

Mathematics is beautiful—and it can be fun and exciting as well as practical. *Good Math* is your guide to some of the most intriguing topics from two thousand years of mathematics: from Egyptian fractions to Turing machines; from the real meaning of numbers to proof trees, group symmetry, and mechanical computation. If you've ever wondered what lay beyond the proofs you struggled to complete in high school geometry, or what limits the capabilities of the computer on your desk, this is the book for you.

Mark C. Chu-Carroll
(282 pages) ISBN: 9781937785338. $34
https://pragprog.com/book/mcmath

The Healthy Programmer

To keep doing what you love, you need to maintain your own systems, not just the ones you write code for. Regular exercise and proper nutrition help you learn, remember, concentrate, and be creative—skills critical to doing your job well. Learn how to change your work habits, master exercises that make working at a computer more comfortable, and develop a plan to keep fit, healthy, and sharp for years to come.

This book is intended only as an informative guide for those wishing to know more about health issues. In no way is this book intended to replace, countermand, or conflict with the advice given to you by your own healthcare provider including Physician, Nurse Practitioner, Physician Assistant, Registered Dietician, and other licensed professionals.

Joe Kutner
(254 pages) ISBN: 9781937785314. $36
https://pragprog.com/book/jkthp

The Pragmatic Bookshelf

The Pragmatic Bookshelf features books written by developers for developers. The titles continue the well-known Pragmatic Programmer style and continue to garner awards and rave reviews. As development gets more and more difficult, the Pragmatic Programmers will be there with more titles and products to help you stay on top of your game.

Visit Us Online

This Book's Home Page
https://pragprog.com/book/javacomp
Source code from this book, errata, and other resources. Come give us feedback, too!

Keep Up to Date
https://pragprog.com
Join our announcement mailing list (low volume) or follow us on twitter @pragprog for new titles, sales, coupons, hot tips, and more.

New and Noteworthy
https://pragprog.com/news
Check out the latest pragmatic developments, new titles and other offerings.

Save on the eBook

Save on the eBook versions of this title. Owning the paper version of this book entitles you to purchase the electronic versions at a terrific discount.

PDFs are great for carrying around on your laptop—they are hyperlinked, have color, and are fully searchable. Most titles are also available for the iPhone and iPod touch, Amazon Kindle, and other popular e-book readers.

Buy now at *https://pragprog.com/coupon*

Contact Us

Online Orders: *https://pragprog.com/catalog*
Customer Service: *support@pragprog.com*
International Rights: *translations@pragprog.com*
Academic Use: *academic@pragprog.com*
Write for Us: *http://write-for-us.pragprog.com*
Or Call: +1 800-699-7764